- You want ~~i~~ _____ned understanding about the industry you are about to enter

- You are about to start your life as an actor and don't know where to begin

- You want to gain a comprehensive overview of which drama schools are right for you

- You want to learn body language techniques giving you instant confidence banishing pre-audition nerves

- You want to create a rock solid emotional foundation stone upon which to build your career

- You want to learn the secret of how to strike instant rapport at auditions without saying a word

- You want to learn how to help your agent to get you more auditions from top London agent Bill Petrie

- You want to learn what to expect when you audition for screen, theatre and musicals

How to Audition Your Way to Success

by

Paul Ryan
and
Richard Williams

© **Improve On You 2016**

If you have received this book from a third party, please note all rights are reserved by Paul Ryan on behalf of Improve On You. No part of this publication may be reproduced, stored in a retrieval system or transmitted in any form or by any means electronic, mechanical, photocopying, recording or otherwise, without prior written permission of Paul Ryan at Improve On You.

Dedications

From Paul

This book is fondly dedicated to Rosie Onyett and John Boylan, the teachers who gave me all I needed and so much more to go into the acting profession – a life full of thanks for my lifelong career.

From Richard

For Joanna.

Contents

- About the authors
- Introduction

Part One

Laying the foundations of your career

In this chapter you will gain an insight into the state of the entertainment industry, how often actors work, how much they get paid and how likely you are to stay in the business.

In this chapter you will learn the value of choosing a 'second string' that will enhance you as a person and as an actor.

In this chapter you will learn to take stock of your roots as a performer thus far and develop an emotional compass and moral foundation stone that you will need as an actor.

Part 3
Relaxation, Rapport, Results!

Chapter 8   p100
Waiting for an audition

In this chapter you will learn how to use a combination of highly potent body language tools to create self-assurance and clarity of mind as you wait to go in to your audition.

Chapter 9   p107
The value of a great first impression

In this chapter you will learn where the true power of how we communicate actually lies. You will learn how to have your audition panel following your emotional lead and how to create a first impression that is positive and lasting so that you will get seen again and again.

Chapter 10   p116
How best to press the flesh

In this chapter you will learn the best way to shake the hand of all those on an audition panel to guarantee you win their confidence and trust instantly.

Chapter 11
In your own time

In this chapter you will learn a variety of powerful non verbal communication techniques that will give you confidence as you stand in front of the audition panel waiting for the onset of your song, speech or reading.

Chapter 12
How to handle a re-call

In this chapter you will learn how to handle the higher anxiety levels that come into play when you get closer to the job...and the money.

Part 4
The business of 'show business'

Chapter 13
Agents

In this chapter you will learn how to chose an agent, how to enhance your agent's ability to get you seen and how to cultivate a positive working relationship with them.

Chapter 14   p185

Auditioning for musicals

In this chapter you will learn the specific demands of the musical theatre audition from West End star Linzi Hateley.

Chapter 15   p194

Auditioning for screen

Two of our most successful and enduring screen actors, Joseph Millson and Karen Henthorn share a host of brilliant insights and techniques to help put you in the right place for a screen audition.

Chapter 16   p214

Auditioning for theatre

Richard Williams talks about what traps to avoid when being seen for a theatre production.

Chapter 17   p227

Auditioning for commercials

In this chapter you will learn the key elements for always giving a great commercial audition and stand out from the crowd.

Epilogue   p236

Final thoughts and good wishes.

About the authors

Paul Ryan

Paul's background is placed firmly in the theatre. He was a child actor performing in the West End at the tender age of 13 back in 1978. Since that time he has appeared in more than 65 productions, 40 or so commercials and a smattering of TV shows. He has written two plays, 'Come To Papa' and 'Six Naughty Kittens' also the book and lyrics to the musical 'Sadly Solo Joe' which was mounted at The Greenwich Theatre and went on to be the flagship production at The Festival of New Musicals.

As a second string to his bow Paul moved into the world of corporate training and in 2012 he set up his own business, Improve On You.

Since that time Paul has developed Improve On You workshops in presentation skills, confidence building and open communication and has taken those into small businesses and international corporations. He also runs an audition technique masterclass at The Drama Centre London, The Midlands Academy of Dance and Drama and The Royal Academy of Music.

Richard Williams

Richard has auditioned thousands of actors during a professional career as a director spanning 30 years. His work has encompassed Shakespeare, including Hamlet at Elsinore Castle, new plays, West End and national and international touring productions.

He has been artistic director of four varied and important regional theatres – Contact Theatre Manchester, Oxford Stage Company, Unicorn Theatre London and Liverpool Playhouse. He has worked with a huge range of acting talents from the immediately recognizable – Roger Allam, Imelda Staunton, Kevin Whateley, David Thelfall – through to wonderfully gifted performers whose names are not well known though their talent is unquestionable.

Richard has been course director of the Foundation Studies in Performance at Drama Centre London for the past nine years and his students have had outstanding success in gaining places on BA courses at all of the recognized drama schools in the UK.

Introduction

Who the hell am I to say that what you will learn from this book will bring you 'success' as an actor? After all what is success, what is it to be an actor and how the hell do you get an audition in the first place?

First things first then, I think it will be a helpful exercise to break down the title of this book to its component parts to best frame and manage your expectations from, possibly, the first ever £10 you have invested in your career. The best way of doing this is in reverse. Let's start with...

How to Audition Your Way To 'Success'

What do I mean by 'success'?

Success comes in various degrees of course. None of you have heard of me. I'm not famous in the traditional sense of the word, I'm not a celebrity, and I'm not even well known 'within the business' yet I still consider myself a successful actor.

For a start off I made my professional debut in 1978 and, through thick and often very thin, have been working as an actor ever since.

This book is full of hard facts about the acting game. The first one is that most drama school students don't last five years in the business once they have graduated. At the time of writing I've been in the game for 38 years which means my career spans five decades. There's comparative success in that straight away.

In that time I have been in more than 70 productions covering Shakespeare, Moliere, Brecht, and Mozart. I have performed in the West End, the fringe, arts festivals, number one tours travelling the length and breadth of the country, and a clutch of our, now sadly, dwindling rep theatres. I have written a musical – and had it produced. I have directed plays, opera and children's shows. I have appeared in more than 40 commercials, done voice over work, radio plays and over the years made a number of guest appearances in countless TV shows here in the UK and across the water.

I know when I first set out I wanted to achieve far more than all that I have put forward in the above list – in short, I wanted to be a star. That hasn't happened (yet!) but looking back with a greater understanding of the business and all its vicissitudes I can say with a huge degree of satisfaction that I have become, at the very least, a seasoned professional. If being one of those represents success as an actor to you then read on and know you are in safe and experienced hands.

How To Audition 'Your Way' To Success

How exciting to know that you stand at the very beginning of the most amazing and unique journey in your life as an actor. No two careers are the same so the way you choose to travel through the profession really is 'your way' and yours alone.

No matter how hard others may try to push you into a mould or see you as a particular type, your individuality can never be taken away from you. True, you may well fit a certain profile in the way you are cast; your age, sex and look makes that highly probable, but how you decide to manoeuvre your way through the minefield of choices, the maze of situations and the myriad of personalities you will come up against is ultimately up to you.

Make no mistake about it; the world of the performing arts will be breathtaking at both ends of the spectrum. When things go well, it will be breathtakingly euphoric but when things go badly it will be breathtakingly frustrating, maddening and heartbreaking. Part of 'your way' will be how you deal with the highs and lows of this most exciting yet unpredictable, rewarding yet unjust of vocations.

The good times are easy. The bad times are hard. As actors we can swing violently between these two situations and they can come hotter on the heels of one another than you could possibly give credit for. I have often made good choices as an actor but more often bad choices as an unemployed actor.

I aim to give you insights into how to deal with the bad times when they come and how to use the good times to their best effect to keep you going when the bad times happen again so that ultimately the good times will make a welcome return once more. This is the topography of acting. For most of us it undulates quite violently.

To paraphrase the great Bette Davis, 'Fasten your seat belts, it's going to be a bumpy ride'.

How To 'Audition' Your Way To Success

This part of the breakdown is easy, a simple definition will suffice:

audition |ôˈdiSHən|

noun

an interview for a particular role or job as a singer, actor, dancer, or musician, consisting of a practical demonstration of the candidate's suitability and skill.

verb [no obj.]

perform an audition: *he was* **auditioning for** *the lead role in the play.*

• [with obj.] assess the suitability of (someone) for a role by means of an audition: *she was* **auditioning** *people for* her *new series.*

Actually, a simple definition won't suffice

The process you go through when you audition for a theatre job will be very different from when you are seen for a commercial casting. Musical theatre auditions are particularly taxing, not least because of the singing and dancing element but also the sometimes seemingly endless rounds of recalls you are put through before you are cast.

Auditions for TV and film are different again - the new kid on the block here is the 'self tape' whereby you stick yourself in front of your smart phone and do a short piece of dialogue which you email direct to the casting director who will submit it to producers once viewed and approved.

I'm guessing, though, that for most of you reading this book the first audition of real meaning that you have yet to experience is the drama school audition. A positive and informed approach to these all-important auditions is utterly essential and for this reason I am co-authoring this book with Richard Williams.

Aside from being one of the country's leading theatre directors of the last 30 years he is also the head of the foundation course at the Drama Centre London. So for chapters pertaining to drama school auditions I hand the reins over to him and later in the book Richard talks about auditioning for theatre.

Through the course of this book we will look at each of the different types of audition scenario you will find yourself in and discuss how best to raise yourself to each particular set of challenges.

'How To' Audition Your Way To Success

Now, here we get to the nitty gritty of why I am writing this book. As I said, I began my career back in the 70s. I was a child actor and started out playing the Artful Dodger in the West End production of 'Oliver!' and from that day to this I have been in the company of actors old and young, all professing with a weary gravitas that 'auditions never get any easier'. Well, for years I agreed with them.

It was a received wisdom that I never challenged. Consequently I always carried a sense of impending doom on the approach to any audition my agent secured for me.

If you believe that 'auditions never get any easier' you are implicitly saying that 'auditions are always hard' and, furthermore, that they will always be so. What a terrible burden to carry along with everything else that makes our choice of career so difficult. It is also a very damaging mindset.

If you audition through nervousness and anxiety you will not be at your best. Mistakes are far more likely to happen, the interview part of an audition will be all sound and fury signifying nothing, your personality may well take a 20 minute break leaving only a nervous husk in its place so any chance of creating a positive first impression are diminished to near zero and you risk walking away knowing that you wasted the opportunity.

For reasons I will explain later, I firmly believe that an audition that went well is never wasted, but a bad audition can hang in your heart for a very long time thereafter, again, producing a toxic negativity to your mindset. This is bound to have a knock on affect to your next audition and you may go through a crisis of confidence.

At the age of 38 I had an epiphany that has altered my whole view on how to approach auditions ever since. It came about as a direct result of teaching presentation skills and confidence-building techniques in the corporate sector and it has stood me in such good stead and made the whole auditioning experience a completely positive one. Since that time I can honestly say, hand on heart that I have never given a bad audition. My head is always in the right place before, during and after an audition and each experience makes me a stronger candidate for the next job I go up for.

The epiphany? Simple...

People who say, 'auditions never get any easier' are wrong!

And through the course of this book I am going to share a whole host of tools to help you approach each audition with the 'can do' attitude that will be your best friend and ally through the course of your career.

The contents of this book are based on the audition technique master class that I run each year at the Drama Centre London. I always make a start by telling the students that I am about to really p#ss them off. And in chapters one, two and three I'm fairly sure I'm about to really p#ss you off too. Why?- Because I'm going to hit you with all the bad news upfront.

I feel it is essential to give you an informed overview into what you can expect from the acting game right from the word go. For this reason the first few chapters are the 'telling it like it is' bit. It makes for fairly gloomy reading in some respects but once you get to chapter four we start to concentrate on what is great about being an actor and begin the process of equipping you with a wide range of methods and techniques to enhance your ability to give a great audition every time.

Enjoy.

'Graduates, you made it! And now... you're f#cked!'
- Robert De Niro addressing graduates of the NYU Tisch School of the Arts

Chapter 1

What are the odds?

Make no mistake about it, the one thing you will have to overcome every day of your career are the odds!

But what are the odds and how heavily are they stacked against you?

I'm sure you are keenly aware of how hard it is in the entertainment industry but is it really all that bad? I mean, there *is* plenty of work and plenty of people *in* work. It's out there, it does actually *exist* so why am I labouring so hard to point out the overall paucity of opportunities? Am I just a bitter, grumpy old bastard intent on putting off as many of you as possible or are Richard and I two kindly souls making an effort to be as rigorously honest about the situation so that you have been properly warned? It's the latter.

And I've got the stats to back us up...

You have probably heard the old saying that most actors only work for a third of any given year. Well, as I started to put this chapter together I had this nagging suspicion that the old 'third of a year' thing might no longer be true so I asked actress and trade union activist for Equity Nicola Hawkins if she could give me a more up to date overview of employment figures for actors. She very kindly sent over the results of the 2013 Equity members survey and it makes for some quite sobering reading (no surprise there then).

As with all surveys the statistics that get thrown up can be interpreted in many different ways but if you are happy with me painting in broad strokes I think there are some key insights worthy of your consideration.

3,804 Equity members took part in the survey and the percentages are based on that. Worth noting perhaps that most straw polls are based on far fewer people, often just 100, so the information given has helped to create a hugely comprehensive outline of the state of the game regarding both employment levels and rates of pay.

What I'm out to establish is how likely you are to get work and how likely you are to be able to live off what you earn from that work.

Here we go...

Gender split:

Of those surveyed 53.5% were male, 46.1% were female and 0.4% transgender.

This is interesting for a number of reasons. I was surprised to learn that there are more men in the profession than women. This is not something that has ever been reflected in the gender split in any drama class that I have had experience in teaching. Indeed, I recently taught a class of 32 students of whom only three were male. Strange then that, in truth, there are more men than women. This is helpful for women because as there is so little work for 'ladies of a certain age' at least there are less of you out there fighting over what there is available to you when you hit your 40s.

How long people stick at it:

When asked how long people had been members of Equity those who had been members for less than five years made up 24.6% and those who had been members for more than 25 years made up 29.9%.

This seems to indicate that you have about 27% chance of sticking to the business for life. I think this is far more heartening than it might first appear. One in three will stay with acting as their career, which considering just how challenging the profession is it's pretty good going and a real testament to the doggedness and commitment of performers in general.

What about the work!

If you have a drink near to hand I suggest you take a slug of it right now.

Let me give you exactly what was put into the published

results and we'll spend some time dissecting them after you've had a chance to digest them.

The question asked was, 'How many weeks professional work did you undertake in the last 12 months?'

The answers were as follows:

None	10.5%
Less than 10 weeks	34.9%
10 to 20 weeks	20.1%
20 to 30 weeks	13.3%
30 to 40 weeks	9.0%
More than 40 weeks	12.1%

Just as I suspected, a quick glance at this list tells me we certainly need to review the 'third of a year' assertion. I'm afraid it's much more bleak than that. It's not quite as pithy a phrase but try this for an amended reality check:

In any given year nearly half of all actors will either work for just two-and-a-half months or not at all

Bloody hell!

If you think this is bad, wait till I tell you about the money!

Whether we like these figures or not it does help to focus on how very important it is for you to choose a second career to go hand-in-hand with your life as an actor.

There is a phrase that I first heard from a friend of mine, Jeffery Harmer. We lived in a house crammed full of actors in Crouch End. At that time some were doing fabulously well while others like Jeffry and I were struggling. One time I was having a bitch about not having a job and he stopped me by saying, 'But Paul, you do really well! Of course there are hard times but you're like me. I work more than most, not as often as some' which made me feel instantly better.

'More than most, not as often as some'

It is a phrase that I have taken great comfort in ever since. And looking at the results from the Equity survey, if you get one good job of reasonable length in a year you will be able to say that about yourself!

Of course you want more and I hope you get it. Should you not, it might help put things into perspective to remember that there are plenty out there who are worse off than you.

And on the upside 29.4% of us will be in work most of the time. It would be fascinating to know how these figures stack up against say 20 years ago. But given the state of the business as it is today I think that we should take heart in this. If you work half the year you are doing very well. Anything beyond that and you are doing very well indeed and should count your blessings.

Show me the money!

Er... I'd take another gulp out of that drink (if you can afford it!)

Check this out. Regarding actor's pay the question put was:

How much did you earn from your work in the entertainment industry in the past 12 months?

Here's what came out of the survey.

Nothing	11.2%
Under 5K	37.7%
£5K to £10K	18.3%
£10K to £20K	19.1%
£20K to £50K	11.4%
£50K to £100K	1.5%
Over 100K	0.7%

Rather tellingly 263 people who filled out the survey chose not to answer this question. I'm guessing they were people who earned too little and didn't want to admit it or who earned too much and felt it was none of our ruddy business actually, thank you very much indeed.

Either way, there is more than enough data to drawer some highly significant conclusions. The main one being that, if you want to earn a decent wage, as Robert De Niro so gently put it 'you're fucked'. It's pretty bleak isn't it? I mean I knew we had it tough but this is taking the piss.

Firstly, no surprise that the 10% or so who didn't work also failed to earn anything. Awful for them but in fairness many people from all walks of life suffer unemployment at one time or another. We don't hold the copyright on suffering – it just feels like we do.

Then I think it gets a lot darker with the terrible fact that just under 38% of actors earn less than £5,000 a year. Staggering.

Things remain bleak in the extreme for the next earning bracket. 18.3% only earn between five and ten thousand. Even at the top end of that you are coming in at £192.30 a week, a dismal £32 a day (£4 an hour) So 56% of us earn less than the minimum wage as performers.

God almighty, let's make an effort to cheer ourselves up a bit shall we.

19.1% are saying they earn between ten and twenty thousand annually. Good; things are finally starting to look a bit more sensible. Twenty grand sounds like quite a good sum of money actually. But take a moment to think about how you are going to make that last over a year. £20,000 breaks down to £384.61 a week or £8 per hour.

If you happen to be based in London and living in rented accommodation you'll know all to well more than half of that will be eaten up just by paying for a place to live.

The biggest conclusion from all the data is this:

Only 13.6% of performers can actually claim to make a living from acting.

And if I'm honest I think even that is stretching it.

The difference between twenty and fifty thousand pounds is huge and I'm guessing that the majority of people who ticked the box for that earning category will have been on the lower end of the scale and would therefore be struggling to make ends meet.

Either way the majority of us are following our passion while subsidising the arts and making countless other untold sacrifices to stay in the business of acting – 'cos there ain't no money!

That's the coffee. Now wake up and smell it!

Chapter 2

What else can you do?

Given all that we have learnt about the state of the business in the previous chapter you may be surprised to learn that I am not going to go onto the whole, 'are you sure this is what you really want to do?' thing. Nor am I going to say that you should only consider a life on the stage if you absolutely 'have' to act. (I'll leave that to Richard).

I am making the assumption that you are burning to get on stage and do your thing; that it is the only thing you give a damn about, the only thing you want to do and the only thing you can see yourself doing. If you have this kind of manic zeal about becoming an actor then you are equipped with the blind passion necessary to help you brazen your way through the first set of hurdles you are likely to come across.

At this early stage in proceedings I want to discuss one of those hurdles with you before we really get going on the main thrust of the book.

I was in a play recently and asked a couple of cast members, 'What is the worst thing you can be without as an actor?'

The first actor said 'talent', the second said 'work'.

These are both good answers but in my opinion wrong. Let me deal each of those responses in isolation.

Being without talent

You will learn that, for all its injustices, the acting game has a strangely ironic and even-handed approach to making sure that people with no talent at all will gain employment. It will come most sharply into focus when you fail to get a job that you are dead right for, only to see that the person who secured the role is, in your opinion, TOTALLY BLOODY USELESS!

Not only that but you will also be cast in productions where you will come across people whose lack of ability will draw your breath. It is one of the myriad of challenges we are confronted with. Having to work with someone who, nice as they might be, doesn't have 'it'.

Best approach? Understand that all art is subjective and your opinion is only that – an opinion. I have seen a few in my time who I didn't have much faith in during the rehearsal period only to be greatly surprised when it came to first night. Also, actors take time to mature. Give people the benefit of the doubt, treat them with respect and compassion and know that they, just like you, are chasing their dream.

For my own part, I know that on a couple of occasions when I have felt miscast I will have aroused a certain lack of enthusiasm in my fellow company members. Don't get me wrong, I have always had, even during the dark days, an unshakable belief in my abilities but we can't all be good at everything all the time.

As actors most of us are what is called, in NLP (Neuro Linguistic Programming) terms, 'External Referencers' - we thrive on the praise and positive feedback from others. So if you are ever in a situation where you are working with someone who – in your opinion – isn't all that good, offer them your unstinting support and encouragement. This will help them to continue to grow. Any demonstrated or passive aggressive disapproval will have the opposite affect and you will see them shrink back and take fewer risks. Our trade is a strange one. We depend on each other so massively. If you want to encourage someone to give a greater performance be there for them and don't judge them too harshly.

Being without work

Of course we all want to be in work all the time but that just isn't going to happen so get used to it. And yes, dear reader, this applies to *you*!

Hard fact number two: You *will* be out of work – a great deal.

If you can't take this on board when choosing to enter the profession you will struggle with the reality of the true nature of the beast. It is what we have to come to terms with as we enter the game. Falling into a decline the minute the curtain comes down on the last night of a show will not serve you well, it will make the emotional highs and lows more extreme and ultimately more difficult to cope with.

As we go through this book we will look at ways to embrace being out of work as a positive. It will keep you strong, it will keep you happy and as a result it will keep you in the right emotional place for your next audition.

I think it's worth pointing out that, for me, some of the most fruitful times of learning have come about when I was unemployed. I once had a period of two years with out a job. Yes, you read that correctly, two years.

Having been a child actor I already had my Equity Card at a time when our union was still a closed shop and near impossible to get into. So having failed my drama school auditions (more of that later) I picked myself up and moved to London. I was 18. I enjoyed a fantastic first flush of success in my initial seven years as a 'grown up', ironically playing lots of boy parts, Huckleberry Finn, Edmund in 'The Lion The Witch and the Wardrobe' and Laurie in 'Little Women' to name but a few. I also took on roles where they needed a 'bright young thing' i.e. good fun but shallow. I then had a gorgeous run of tasty parts in some terrific productions, 'Torch Song Trilogy', Brecht's 'The Recruiting Officer', A wonderfully conflicted public school boy in 'The Boundary' culminating in having the privilege of working for the brilliant director, Mike Alfreds playing Clientè in a production of Moliere's 'The Miser' which did a national tour and ended with a four week run at The Young Vic. I was truly gearing up for great things.

And then nothing.

Two years of nothing.

Can you imagine that? A career that had been going from strength to strength suddenly grinding to an abrupt and nonsensical halt for two heartbreaking years. At the start of it of course I had no idea how long my stint in the wilderness was to last so at the beginning I went at it with my usual sense of positive attack.

In the first three months I learnt to drive – but no work came in.

Over the following three or four months I taught myself rudimentary Spanish. A terrific skill, which serves me well to this day but hey, *still* no work...

As the jobless situation continued my emotional state moved from optimistic, to pragmatic. With more time at my disposal I decided to try my hand at stand up comedy, became a karaoke presenter, wrote a screenplay for a short film and even worked abroad in Tenerife as a compere for a variety show in a hotel.

Whilst I was gaining all this incredible life experience though, my pragmatism about being out of work had morphed into bewilderment then to outrage. From outrage it went to furious, to bitter, frustrated, hurt, miserable, desperate, and downcast.

After about 18 months I was at that darkest of all places. My resolve was broken and I lost any confidence that I would ever work again. I stopped doing anything constructive with my time and fell headlong into a state of continual and unabated pessimism. I basically hit the skids, drinking to drown my sorrows and smoking to lift my spirits. I was in a mess.

I fell into a depression, a clinical depression that is, not just a bit sad – medication, therapy – the lot.

You see, I had always defined myself through my work and my identity had always been glued to my aspirations. Work stopped, I all but disappeared and when the hope of work was gone, I disappeared all together.

Through the therapy I found myself again. Sounds corny but it's true. I came off the antidepressants, changed my bad habits and started to look forward with a sturdy determination that soon things would change.

They did.

Eventually, the work came back, but not as I would have expected – I was to play a cat in a Christmas show but at least it was the lead! However, once my 'comeback' gained momentum I realized that all the pain, the self doubt, self loathing, soul searching and sorrow had woken up something in me that I was able to use in every part I was ever to play from that time forward (including the cat). In short I had at last made contact with the dark side of my nature and was able to bring a maturity and depth to my acting that had previously not been at my disposal. I had gone through a period of huge transition, which would not have occurred, but for my long stretch of unemployment.

No, being without work is as much a part of being an actor as being on stage. When it happens you must do your level best to allow the experience to fuel you and always hold in your mind that it *will* pass.

I'll ask the question one more time, 'What is the worst thing you can be without as an actor?' My answer? Money.

Being without money

In any walk of life being without money stinks, but for actors it is imperative that we remain solvent when there is no acting work. We should all have a 'civvi street' job to return to once a show has come to a close -not least because if you are working in the theatre the money is jaw-droppingly low. You won't be able to make any savings while you're in work – when you come out the other side of a production you will be in the same financial state as when you went in. So make sure that financial state is a good one.

What I'm driving at is this...

You will need to get a job... a normal job

(See I told you I'd p#ss you off)

Guess what? Things were better in the old days.

I remember being in school and my social studies teacher, Mr Harvey explaining that the government understood how precarious life in the acting profession was and how most work was on a short contract basis. For these reasons the DHSS went out of their way to ensure that actors shouldn't suffer the hardship of waiting for their benefits. Can you believe it? We were blessed by a department of Health and Social Security that actually had a nationwide policy to fast track dole and housing benefit payments to actors as soon as they fell out of work! Incredible to think of it now isn't it?

We were given enough money to live on with a bit of leeway for the odd treat, plus our rent was paid for us as well. You were literally given 'security'.

Also the business itself was better paid back in the 70s and 80s. I can't help thinking it all went pear-shaped the minute Equity lost its closed-shop status, pay rates took a dive almost immediately. Before then TV engagement fees were very healthy indeed plus when you counted in your repeat fees you earned well. Nowadays? Here's something for you to consider:

A very good friend of mine was cast in one of the top Soaps. He was given a year contract. At last, he thought, easy street – constant work and great money; £500 per episode in which you made an appearance with three episodes going out each week! But get this; the contract was so constructed that his average weekly wage for the year ended up at £275.00 – utterly mind-boggling. There *is* good money to be earned out there but it's a lot harder to come by than ever before.

Adverts were always a great way to earn huge amounts of cash. They would keep you going through the down times – but times change. Now with audience figures refracted around all the numerous TV stations, plus the internet, the big core audience has gone and big payouts have all but dried up.

In the old days a standard amount to expect for a mid scale advertising campaign would be about £5-6,000 and that amount of money went a lot further back then than it does now.

I had a friend who did a McDonald's advert back in the early 80s. He had to take a bite out of a Big Mac while looking longingly at it. They put this into slow motion, added the music from 2001:A Space Odyssey and pushed it onto the airwaves so often that my friend was able to put down the money on a house - £50K!

Another friend did a Christmas advert for the same company a couple of years ago. She played the mum in the commercial, quite a heavily featured role. The ad went out solidly for about a month. She was paid £475.00 all in. Go figure!

In fact money on adverts is now so low that in many cases agents refuse to put their clients up for them. It simply doesn't make financial sense to do so. It just isn't worth the bother!

The point is that as you start your career, whether you are about to audition for drama school or have come out the other side of that experience and are taking your first steps as a working actor – you must find alternative ways of earning a living. This what we used to call the 'second string' to our bow and I know as you are reading this that your skin is crawling at the very thought of doing something that lies outside your immediate ambitions.

Rethink this.

Getting a job will help you to *achieve* your ambitions.

By keeping solvent you will be able to keep your options open and pay for all the expenses you will incur as you set yourself up in the profession. And besides with the current state of affairs you haven't got much of a choice.

I gather from the younger actors I come across nowadays that the time and effort that goes into getting dole and rent makes it a near pointless waste of time. In my view this is all for the good.

Going back to when I first moved to London in 1983 I got my dole money and I got my rent money straight away. Great. Then what did I do? I sat on my big fat neurotic arse and waited for the phone to ring. Bad plan. If you do nothing for long enough you will start to become isolated, anxious and cut yourself away from other people. I hung around in my flat looking at my roommate (another would-be actor) for about six months on and off. Sitting around all day, strapped for cash and heavy with an unexpressed yearning to perform, it didn't take long before we were over exposed to one another. In short we started to get on each other's tits quite badly.

Then a pal of ours moved just around the corner. He was a film student and the first thing he did on arriving in London was to get himself a job at the local Pizza Hut and, thank God, he talked me into getting a job along side him. The difference it made to my daily sense of well-being and attitude was amazing.

I came off the dole – that makes you feel good instantly - I was meeting new people and I had money in my pocket. The wages were ok but the tips were fantastic. Everything seemed brighter. The job also had flexibility. They were happy for me to go off on acting jobs and I had a job waiting for me on my return.

My flat mate resolutely did not get a job. He remained on the dole, remained strapped for cash and remained isolated from the rest of society. Every time he went into an audition he was carrying an incredible sense of desperation with him. We will talk at length later about the first impression you make when you go into an audition room and how vital it is. Certainly, if you go in with a palpable sense of neediness it will turn people off you. He failed to get any work and subsequently turned his back on acting within a year.

So get yourself a job.

In the first instance I would say any job that offers you flexibility and a decent rate of pay. All the traditional jobs that unemployed actors have done down the years are a good place to start. For example, waiting on tables, bar work, being an usher in your local theatre, maybe working at Ticketmaster – they really have an understanding of the need you will have to occasionally drop a shift due to an audition. Be an office temp, try and get into role-play. These jobs are all good for when you are first starting out. Do this. You will have fun, make friends, make money and keep your sanity; while all the time enriching your life experience and broadening your frame of reference.

These sorts of jobs are relatively easy to get, you can leave at the drop of a hat and they are all solid ways of earning while you're waiting for the next contract BUT, and here's the kicker, they are all dead end jobs.

More thought will need to be given to your 'second string' if it is to carry you through the quiet times of your career. The older you get the less satisfied you will be to come out of a show and go to work as a waiter. Your life situation will have changed; there might be a spouse, children, even a mortgage. At that stage a dead end job will be neither good for your levels of self-esteem or sufficiently well paid to keep you in the market to work as an actor.

As I grew older and my status as an adult could no longer be denied (beautiful wife, kids and mortgage) I had to move away from short-term jobs to something more substantial to keep the mortgage paid and keep me free for acting. It's tough but needs must.

I got a job in the corporate training industry with a small company that taught presentation skills. It turned out I was quite good at it so for seven years I was able to run the two jobs together quite harmoniously. I then went into Mamma Mia for three years and halfway through made up my mind that on leaving the show I would set myself up as an independent business trainer.

The long and the short of it was that I created my own company, 'Improve On You'. It's been hard work but the rewards are huge. It has taken time but I now command a healthy day rate and it has enabled me to stay in the business and be more selective in the work I chose to accept. (No more cats!)

With regard to *your* 'second string' I want to you to think of the bigger picture. Assuming you are in the business for the long haul here is a story for you to ponder:

I was working up north a number of years ago doing a two show gig over the Christmas period. I was cross cast as Baron Hard Up in 'Cinderella' and Cannon Chasuble in 'The Importance Of Being Earnest'. One day I was sitting in the green room during a break writing a blog for 'Improve On You' and the actress playing Lady Bracknell plonked herself down next to me with a cup of tea and we started to have a chat.

After a short time she peered at my laptop and asked what I was doing. I explained all about 'Improve On You' and took the liberty of showing her my website (improveonyou.co.uk). She asked me all about it, she looked over my site for quite a while, looking at the videos and other pieces of content I had on there at the time. Eventually she let out a huge sigh and sank back into her chair.

'I wish I could do something like that', she said rather disconsolately. 'But you can', I said hoping to offer some encouragement. 'No', she said, 'it's too late, I've left it too late'. I asked what she did in between jobs. 'I pull pints in my local village pub'. This lady was fifty-six years of age at the time.

Just to explain, this actress had a CV like a side of beef. It dripped with wonderful credits – huge Shakespearian roles at the RSC, numerous and brilliant appearances at the Royal National Theatre, Northern Broadsides and The Manchester Royal Exchange. She also had a long list of very impressive TV appearances to her name the last of which was having been a regular on EastEnders.

She then went on to tell how, once she had come out of EastEnders she was asked by the local school to be the celebrity guest to open the fete that year. She was vey flattered and happy to help. She even had a stack of postcards from her days on EastEnders that she brought along for signing autographs. She said, 'I gave a great speech. I was funny and said all the right things about all the right people. I didn't leave anything out and I opened the fete with a flourish. After I had given out my autograph to any one who wanted it I took a look at my watch and realized my shift was about to start in the pub. When I first went in the place was dead then slowly but surely all the people who had seen me give the speech as a local celebrity started to come into the pub as customers. And I had to serve them their drinks. Go through what flavour crisps we had. Take their money give them their change. It was horrible', she said, 'I brazened it out but it was bloody horrible. Oh how the mighty are fallen'.

I've told that story many times and each time I can see the face of the person listening fall into an anguished cringe. A brilliant and accomplished actress comes out of a national soap opera and gets a job that pays £6.35 an hour.

I asked her why she didn't consider doing something a bit more worthwhile.

'Because I can't do anything else', was her reply.

If I had a pound for every time I've heard an actor say 'I can't do anything else' I'd be as rich as Croesus, I mean *seriously* loaded. What is it about us as a breed that we need to continually denigrate ourselves in such a way?

Listen, if you really did choose to commit to a life in the acting profession because you can't do anything else – do something else. Anything else.

We are not just talented actors, we are talented people. We tend to be expert communicators, bright personalities, magnetic and vibrant with a host of skills that would easily crossover into other jobs. Find something you love, have a true interest and passion that you can put into your secondary career and let it grow through the years into something that feeds your soul and fills your stomach.

There.

Did I manage to p#ss you off?

Will you take any notice?

Probably not.

At the beginning of our careers we simply cannot countenance the fact that we will be ever out of work. I genuinely hope you are one of the lucky few who can carve out a career in the business without needing to do anything else. The likelihood is that you won't be so I'll say it one last time...

You will need to get a job... a normal job!

Chapter 3

Who are you and what are you doing here?

It is one of the most difficult moments you will come across when you go to an audition. All may have gone swimmingly well during your speech, song or reading and you are invited to take a seat and the interviewer drops this on you...

'So tell me about yourself'

It is not strictly a question, more an open invitation for you to let them know all about you while at the same time projecting your personality and ability to communicate. And it has a nasty habit of catching people out.

Hold on a minute, I know what you're thinking...

Where are all the brilliant exercises to do with audition technique? Haven't they missed something out? Why are we jumping right past that part of the process and going straight to the interview bit? Well, the truth is I am still very much in the prepping stage and it is best if you view this next chapter as deep-rooted, foundation-stone preparation, not just for all your auditions, but the rest of your career as well. My God, you can't say this book isn't giving you value for money!

Another hard fact about the acting profession, just in case you didn't know it, is that it is one of the most oversubscribed jobs in the work market. Everybody wants to do it. Yes, it's an existence fraught with a welter of hardships but, at the end of the day, you can't get away from the fact that when you actually get the chance to perform, it is tremendous fun. And because of the sheer volume of people all hoping to do what you are hoping to do – sorry to have to say it but – there will be many who will be just as good, if not actually better than you. (Ouch!)

So what do you have to bring to the table that makes you the ideal candidate? What will make you shine head and shoulders above the rest? What single thing do you have in your possession that makes you the obvious choice? The answer has appeared five times in this paragraph alone.

YOU!

Who you are

What you stand for

And why you're an actor in the first place

In our greatly overcrowded profession you must spend time to consider your USP. By that I mean your unique selling proposition. Being a great actor, excellent singer or mind-blowingly amazing dancer does not make you unique, it only makes you a contender. What every audition or interview ultimately hinges on is whether the people behind the desk want to spend their time with you. In other words, do they like you? I would like to suggest that what actually makes you unique is your personality, your values, your story.

To that end I would like you to spend some time considering what your core values are. When we have an understanding of exactly what our values are we can use them as a prism through which we approach our work and the people we meet through our work. Now, I don't know what your values are of course, that's for you to decide, but in essence you are looking for the best in yourself and as I'm sure you understand if we bring the best of ourselves to any situation, that situation, whatever it is, will be greatly enhanced for both you and those around you.

When the great children's theatre school impresario Anna Scher set up her academy back in the early 70s she did something amazing. Before letting her young charges out into the world she gave them all the most fantastic set of values to work by: Be Prompt, Polite and Professional.

I know this might seem a bit simplistic but these values helped her young students to become highly successful child actors. When you consider the careers that she has launched include Ray Winstone, Martin and Gary Kemp, Pauline Quirke and Linda Robson the proof is in the pudding. I saw Martin Kemp on a chat show speaking about his time at Anna Scher's. What stuck in my mind was when he spoke about the values she had instilled in him as a child. He said, he has used them every day of his working life ever since. 'Whenever I have a job to do I always arrive on time, I'm pleasant to people and do the work to the best of my ability. In short, I'm prompt, polite and professional. Thanks Anna'

For my own part I didn't really know anything about the benefits of knowing one's core values throughout most of my time in the business. Starting my career with nothing but the cockiness of youth bore only so much inner resilience. Despite a great deal of good fortune once the school of hard knocks and the years of perceived disappointments had taken their toll my default values had become:

Despair	Impatience	Longing
Escapism	Blame	Resentment

Then, halfway through my three-year stint in Mamma Mia I studied for a diploma in Neuro Linguistic Programming. One of the first things you learn is to identify your own values so that you gain a greater understanding of who you are and what you stand for. After giving the matter some thought here is what I chose as my core set of values

Discipline	Flexibility	Playfulness
Honesty	Compassion	Courage

Just looking at these two sets of values you can see which are going to have a better and more positive effect on the way I negotiate my way in the world in both the immediate and the long term. Every day I read my list of core values and do my very best to live up to them. As a result I am strengthened in so many ways but particularly when it comes to my approach to the business of acting. To give you a further steer on this let's go through each one of my core values and see how they help me.

Discipline

- Helps me raise myself to every challenge
- Keeps me focused on the job in hand and ensures I give it my all
- Working with discipline helps me to wring out all there is to learn and grow of any situation

Flexibility

- Helps me to be accepting of other people's way of working
- Makes me more receptive to new ideas
- Aids cooperation and collaboration

Playfulness

- Keeps me in the moment
- Makes me less self-censoring therefore more creative
- Makes me fun to be with

Honesty

- Deception wastes time and complicates every situation. Being honest therefore saves me time and keeps things simple
- Helps people to view me as trustworthy and upright
- If I'm honest and tactful with others they will be honest and tactful with me.

Compassionate

- Encourages my ability to listen well and give help

when needed

- Stops me being too judgmental of others
- Makes me sensitive and therefore caring to the needs of other people.

Courage

This is a big one. For every day that I am working, but equally for every day that I am waiting, I draw on my reserves of courage to help me face and sometimes stare down the many challenges I am forced to cope with as an actor. Most days I have bouts of cowardice. By reminding myself of my value of courage, guess what, I feel instantly more courageous.

I am of course just a mere mortal. If I were absolutely all of those things at all times I would either be canonised on my passing or an unbearable goody two-shoes while still alive.

The point of core values is not to turn you into a paragon of virtue but to enhance your resolve and strengthen your moral fibre giving you greater resilience when you face the disappointments the business often throws at you.

Knowing your core values will never turn you into a know-all because your values will teach you there is always more to know

Now it's your turn. I would like you to take some time out and decide what your core values are so that you too can enjoy the benefits of a firm foundation stone to the way you cope with life and the business –whatever they may throw at you.

Choose six values and write down how they affect you, those around you and how you approach the acting profession.

Do this now.

All done?

I hope so.

Read them often. Let them be your guide. You will draw strength from them when you need it – which will be more often than you think.

Along with knowing your values I think there is a real benefit in reminding yourself of the moment you knew you had to do be an actor and the journey you have taken so far in making that a reality. We all know choosing an actor's life takes incredible courage and to remind ourselves of all our successes and mini wins can reawaken our commitment to carry on when the going gets tough.

I'm going to ask you to indulge me for a while I want to go right back to the moment I realised that I wanted to be an actor in the first place. I was very young and even though this realization came to me more than 45 years ago I can still remember it vividly.

I must have been only about five years of age and I was sitting on my mother's knee in the lounge as the whole family was watching a film on the telly. It was a black and white comedy and we were all really enjoying it. Then one of the people on the screen, I think it was Lesley Phillips, did something that made the whole family absolutely roar with laughter. Seeing it in my mind's eye now is a sight that still fills me with an incredible joy – a sofa full of children rocking back and forth with unalloyed hilarity. The noise of all the laughing and the expressions on the faces of my brothers and sisters as they giggled struck a massive chord in me.

I looked round at my Mum and, pointing to the screen, said to her, 'What's he doing Mummy?' My mum smiled down at me, 'Well, he's being funny dear'. But it wasn't the answer that I was looking for, 'No, what's he *doing*? What *is* he?' 'Oh', she said breezily, 'He's an actor dear'. An *actor*! Even the word itself sounded laden with the promise of excitement. Without a flash of hesitation I said, 'I want to be one of those'. My mum was delighted by her little lad professing such a lofty ambition and told the whole family there and then, 'Pauli's going to be an actor everyone'. And thus it was. It became a sort of self fulfilling prophesy in a way. My mum loved introducing me to people who would visit the house and say, 'This is Pauli, he wants to be an actor, don't you dear?' And at everyone's behest I would start 'acting' for them there and then. Pretending to be 'happy', 'strong', 'weak', 'brave'. The more I did this silly sort of thing the more I wanted to do it. I was suddenly getting laughs of my own – I was being funny!

It is interesting to me now that laughter was the spur to my epiphany. I have always loved performing comedy and have to this day delighted in bringing laughter to an audience. It's probably what I'm best at.

When I give in to the occasional burst of naval gazing or self-analysis I sometimes think that putting my head above the parapet in this way was simply a mechanism for getting attention from my overstretched and overworked parents. I was one of six children and being fifth down the line put me in a strange kind of no-man's-land in my Mum and Dad's affections. I was merely one of a large number of offspring and at that stage by far the quietest of the brood. In essence, being funny got me noticed, and being noticed felt really good.

The first 'real world' confirmation that I might actually have something as a performer came a few years later when I was about eight years of age.

I had always been a slightly invisible child at school only notable for not being very good at anything when it came to actual learning. So, guess what? – I compensated for my intellectual shortcomings and sated my need for attention at the same time by becoming the class clown and bigmouth. This will ring bells with many of you reading this book, I know. I started by showing off a bit and then, as I got older, showing off a lot. I probably became a something of a nuisance but, hopefully, not so disruptive that I became a problem.

One afternoon towards the end of term my primary school teacher, Mrs Cale, had a spare hour to fill at the end of the day and suggested an impromptu talent competition. I absolutely jumped at the chance of joining in. Over the preceding few years I had I developed quite a skill for mimicry. There was a

TV impressionist called Mike Yarwood who was all the rage back then and I practically stole his act. Whatever he did, I did, so I got up and basically performed his routine that included a roster of early 70s celebrities including Frank Spencer, David Frost, Malcolm Muggerage, Steptoe and Son and Max Wall.

I had the audience of my contemporaries in the very palm of my hand. The laughter rang out so resolutely around the school building that other teachers were peering in to see what all the commotion was about. Having brought the house down I was then asked to do it all again in front of another class. A command performance! Holy Mother of God! I had ARRIVED! From this point there would be no turning back.

After that it was a fairly standard introduction to performing in all the various end of term productions. I gave my 'Tom Tom, The Piper's Son', I was a 'Light' in the nativity and ended my primary school acting career to huge critical acclaim as Nogbad The Bad in 'Noggin The Nog'. Then I moved up to Hinchinbrooke Secondary with my sights firmly set on the glamour of the lower school play.

Most of us, if not all, will have at least one of our school teachers to thank for putting enough faith in our raw ability to encourage us to go for it in the professional world. I was blessed with an English and drama teacher called Mike Watson who helped me grow as an actor during two major school productions. First when I played the title role in 'Tom Sawyer' and then 'Chunter Hodges' in 'The Life And Times Of Gervaise Beckett' a year later.

Early into my year nine Mr Watson (God forgive me for saying it) made the observation that I was not being sufficiently stimulated by the drama classes he was providing at school. He realised I was getting bored and switching off during class. He took it on his own back to try and find an environment that would be stretching, challenging yet still enjoyable for me.

He contacted a lady called Rosie Onyett who ran the local council-funded drama club that had the wonderfully evocative title of 'The Huntingdon County Youth Theatre Workshop' or 'HYT' for short. Mr Watson explained that he had a young lad of 13 who he thought showed potential. I was two years younger than the entry age of 15 so Rosie would really be taking a huge punt by accepting me. Happily, she did and her decision to do so proved to be a pivotal moment in my life.

Rosie, working in close partnership with head of drama for the county, John Boylan had created something really quite amazing with the 'HYT'. Suffice it to say, it was an experience that has formed the foundation stone of my life as an actor. Every one of my days is touched and informed by my time under Rosie and John's masterful tutelage. I've never won an award and I'm only sorry about that because I always hoped to take the opportunity to thank them both publicly for all that they did for me.

(NB Actually, I *have* won an award, come to think of it. It was for 'Best Comedy Performance' in the French TV Commercial Awards but I couldn't go to the ceremony so it was an opportunity lost. Next time!)

During my time with the HYT I managed to land an audition for the part of The Artful Dodger in the West End production of Oliver and blow me down if I didn't get the job. I then did couple of years in Grange Hill – don't get too excited, I only had about four lines! It was a fantastic way to start in showbiz and I even got my Equity Card into the bargain. But, brilliant as all that hands-on performing experience was, my real growth as an actor was happening back at home with the HYT. I stayed for four years. In that time they took a reasonably talented oik and crafted him into a solid young actor who, at the age of seventeen, was ready to take his drama school auditions.

And that's where the trouble started.

Chapter 4

Know your sh#t!

I'm told that vulnerability is very 'a la mode' right now. If you share your weaknesses people will identify with you and be more prepared to go on your learning journey with you. Well try this: In one way or another I screwed up each and every one of my drama school auditions. Please learn from my mistakes and don't allow what happened to me, to happen to you.

But how did I allow this to happen to me in the first place? What were the reasons behind my fully comprehensive failure?

At risk of sounding like I am making a huge list of mitigating circumstances (I promise I'm not) I feel the need to point out that the idea of going to drama school was not my own. My Mum, who had been such a powerhouse of support and commitment whilst I was in 'Oliver!' was very keen for me to go down the formal training route whereas I wasn't so sure. I already had some professional experience and was the proud possessor of an Equity Card (which back then made Willie Wonka's Golden Ticket look like a piece of second hand toilet paper). Technically, there was nothing to stop me from just getting out there and getting on with it and being young, impatient and omnipotent that was really what I wanted to do.

Now, looking back I see where my Mum was coming from completely but back then I had no real enthusiasm for going to drama school when I could actually just be working. It wasn't just Mum who wanted me go to drama school but Rosie Onyett and John Boylan both urged me to take that path as well. Indeed, as head of drama for the county John was ready to rubber stamp a full education grant for my whole three years, including living expenses – my God! Free tertiary education, those were the days. (The whole country had a lot more money back then and a healthy interest in supporting the arts).

In the face of all that good advice from the people who had been so integral in getting me that far as an actor I basically went along with it to please them. But my efforts were half-hearted to say the least. And here is the first point that I am driving towards: If you are auditioning for drama school to fulfil someone else's wish my best advice is don't do it. You will never go at it with the full attack and commitment needed. Save yourself the trouble and the expense. Sit quietly for as long as you need to focus on what you want for yourself, not what somebody wants for you. You know best on this one.

So with a heavy sense of responsibility for other people's aspirations I put every penny I earned aside for my audition fees and travel expenses, rolled up my sleeves and threw my hat disconsolately into the ring.

In all fairness to myself the first drama school audition went pretty well – that's if you ignore the fact that I went to a party the night before and stupidly chose to hitchhike into London the next day with my fingers crossed that I would get there on time. How ridiculous when I think about it now!

Guildhall School of Speech and Drama held an all day audition split into two parts. First a shared movement and drama workshop with everybody joining in and then the individual auditions where we would perform our speeches. My stupid decision to hitchhike had luckily paid off and once I had settled myself, I actually had a really great experience.

In among the 30 or so others auditioning I met a couple of really nice people, Bill Petrie and Rachel Fielding. With the intensity of the situation we bonded like superglue and during the open drama workshop we helped each other along and relied on each other for moral support. There was a terrific energy in the room as we were all asked to interpret a piece of music as though we were experiencing a state of ecstasy and there was a great deal of laughter too as we all joined in some improvisation exercises.

The class came to an end and then came the individual auditions part of the day. As you might imagine, it suddenly all got rather serious rather quickly.

As we waited we were all given cards with numbers on and told to go through when our number was called out.

I was given the number 13!

It sort of stood as an emblem for the whole of my drama school audition period really. Having said that, I gave a competent couple of speeches – Puck from 'A Midsummer Night's Dream' and Constantine from Chekov's 'The Seagull'. I came out of the other side of my audition feeling very happy with how it all went.

Afterwards I sat with everybody else and waited for the other auditionees to have their go before being told the interview panel's decision. They would be telling us at the end of the day who would be going through to the next round. It was all very exciting, but emotionally rather draining too.

My brand new best friends, Bill and Rachel, and I sat together nervously chatting and laughing our way through any awkward silences. We took the opportunity to exchange addresses while doing our best to act as nonchalantly as possible – hoping to fool each other that we were too cool for school but rather more hoping to fool ourselves.

The wait continued, the laughter stopped. The wait

continued to continue and a silence befell the room as all the applicants became lost in their own thoughts.

Suddenly the door opened and one of the assistants came through with the results.

We all sat bolt upright and beamed bright, desperate and optimistic smiles. A number of names were called out. These names did not include Bill, Rachel or me. Numbness and shock, disappointment and disbelief. As quickly as possible we said our goodbyes and fled into the solace of solitude.

This outcome had never occurred to me as even the most remote possibility. I didn't get in?! Wait a minute, sorry, what? But I was born for this. I'd done all right in there. I had been good, I had been solid and I had been funny.

I went home in a daze and shamefacedly told my family the news. I went to my room and I did the worst thing I could possibly have done under the circumstances; I sulked.

I brooded for days and failed to come to terms with what had happened. I took the rejection personally and my feelings had been terribly hurt. My confidence had been rocked and my enthusiasm and focus for the whole bloody enterprise had been all but extinguished.

I had failed.

But that wasn't true. The simple fact was that I just hadn't got through the first round of the first of my drama school auditions but I couldn't see it in any other way other than as a humiliating failure and it was that mindset that was to be my undoing.

I think part of the reason I had taken the knock back from Guildhall so badly was up until that point I had never countenanced the idea of not getting in. While I don't want any of you to start out with a negative mindset I do want to say that the chances of you being accepted by every school you go for are nil. If you can get your head around this at the outset then when a rejection comes you will be better equipped to see it as part and parcel of the whole experience.

Where I *did* fail was in not being able to pick myself up and continue bloodied but unbowed. A rejection from a drama school audition is best viewed as a wound that will one day be a battle scar not a fatal blow that signals the end of your fight to win through.

As a result of my inability to take a more circumspect view of not getting into Guildhall I took a weighty pessimism with me to all four of my remaining auditions. LAMDA, Webber Douglas, Central and The Drama Centre. Each one was a disaster. I was fretful, resentful and, crucially, underprepared for all of them. I would see the audition going badly and get myself into a terribly negative headspace. I would sit hunched over and nervous as I waited to go in and, I blush as I tell you that in each of the auditions, I forgot my lines.

My ever so fragile ego had taken such a bashing after my first rejection that I never recovered my mojo. After receiving four rejection letters through the post that was it. I had got what I wanted. I wasn't going to drama school. Well done me!

The only things I had as a positive from the whole experience were the addresses of Bill and Rachel. They became my pen pals for the next year or so. They were to provide me with an amazing object lesson in how to keep going until you get what you want.

Through staying in touch with them I later found out that Rachel pushed on in her auditions with focus and commitment and went on to train at The Bristol Old Vic theatre school. Since that time she has enjoyed fantastic theatre, TV and film success including such credits as Cold Feet, This Life, New Tricks, Holby City and Heartbeat. My other pen pal; Bill also kept his head together and eventually got into Webber Douglas. He too had a great time working as an actor until...well, more about Bill later.

While it hurt like hell at the time, I have never had a granule of regret about not going to drama school. Let me get this straight. I think there are a huge amount of positives in getting a formal training and I think that going to drama school is a hugely beneficial way to go into the profession and gaining bucket-loads of performing experience. Also, through the exposure gained from the graduation show, you have a much stronger chance of getting an agent.

But it is not the only way. I am proof of that.

The one thing you need as you go through your time in the business is the resolve to face countless rejections and still have the strength of mind to carry on until you eventually triumph.

Certainly during my drama school auditions my resolve

crumbled. I came away with a heavy heart and a great deal to think about. But one thing that was never in doubt was my desire to be on stage. I crept into my cave for a while, licked my wounds, hatched a plan and slowly recovered my self-confidence. I still had my Equity card after all. I *could* still just go out there and do it.

Which is what I did.

The plan I hatched was to move to London and get an agent. For the next six months I worked as a TV extra and a waiter saving as much money as I could to put down a deposit on a rented flat with a mate from the HYT who was moving to London at the same time. I left home at the age of 18 with nothing but a heart full of hope. I got an agent through the skin of my teeth by pounding the streets and literally knocking on doors to be seen. The speeches I had learnt for my drama school auditions came to my rescue – yes, I'd finally learnt them – as I used them to prove my worth to Bill Ellis of A&B personal management. On the strength of them he took me on and I was his client for the next seven years.

So remember, if you audition well and don't get in this year there is always next year and if you give up on going to drama school that is no reason to give up on your dreams.

Richard is about to give you a fully rounded description of all that you can expect from your experience in auditioning for drama school but before you start the next few chapters there is one thing I have to insist upon you – one rule that you must observe.

If you fail to stick to this rule all the good advice and expert insight that Richard has to offer will be wasted. None of it will have any meaning or worth to you.

Know your sh#t!
By which I mean…

Learn your lines!

I know it seems lame of me to point out the absolute basic requirement for going in and giving of your best but there are a thousand reasons why you may not equip yourself with a totally comprehensive, inside out and back to front knowledge of your lines. The biggest one is procrastination. We always think there will be enough time so we tend to put off doing our lines until we absolutely have to get round to learning the damn things.

But how much time is enough time?

I went about learning my lines only when I felt a small sense of alarm going off in my stomach as the date of my audition approached. Too late! I was learning in haste, nothing really went in, I was always anxious as I tried to get them into my head and as a result that anxiety was always present when I went in to the audition room. It is no surprise then that with my lack of preparation and the massive pressure of the audition situation my lines fled from me at rapid speed – just awful.

And it is something that happens more often than you would

give credit for.

There is a wonderful film called 'Shine' that has a fabulous lesson for all actors with regards to line learning. The film tells the story of concert pianist David Helfgott and his struggle back from the brink of insanity to playing once again on the international music stage.

In one of the early scenes Helfgott is in a one-to-one master class with a venerated classical pianist Cecil Parks, played by John Gielgud. As the young Helfgott nervously fingers the keys of his piano and frustrated by his efforts Parks stops him. 'David, David, David. The first thing you must do when you play the piano is learn the notes. You must learn the notes and then forget them'. David replies, 'So I learn the notes and then I forget them. Why?', to which Parks replied, 'So you can play them, David. So you can play them'.

It's the same thing with your lines. Learn them so rigorously that they go deep into your subconscious memory. Then you will be able to say them a thousand times in a thousand different ways. Say them to yourself regularly and often. Really kick them about. Say them quietly, loudly, angrily, when you're going on a run, doing the dishes or brushing your teeth. Say them in your dreams! Believe me, you simply cannot be too familiar with these speeches.

On the day your body will be flushing so many stress hormones around your body that rational thinking may well go out of the window. If your lines are embedded on to your DNA they will be with you from the beginning of your speech right through to the end.

NB On the subject of anxiety reduction fear not, I will be taking you through a plethora of techniques to steady yourself on the day of your audition. Having said that, I'm sure you will appreciate, there is no point in calmly and confidently walking into your auditions only for you to dry like a bone because you don't have full mastery over your text. So, once more, just for the record...

Learn Your Lines

Part Two

Drama School Auditions

At this point in the proceedings I would like to hand over to my co-author, theatre director Richard Williams. Not only has he held auditions for more than 200 of his own productions, but he is currently director of the foundation course at The Drama Centre London. For these reasons he is eminently qualified to give his advice both on auditioning for drama schools as well as providing valuable insights for experienced actors.

Over to you Richard...

Chapter Five

Applying for drama school

Why do you want to audition anyway?

You must be clear about why you want to audition for drama school, which means you must be clear about why you want to be an actor. What do you want to say as an actor? What kind of actor do you want to be?

Stop and really start to think about it. What have actors given you through their work? We'll come back to this later. Onwards!

Let's take it in chronological order. You've set your mind on applying for drama school so you take a look at their prospectuses on their websites. There are a confusing number of schools so I have listed all the ones you should be thinking of applying to later on in this chapter.

You'll have now discovered that most of the schools are in London, and of course London is the theatre capital of the world, and a magnet for performers of every sort. However there are wonderful teachers and courses outside London as well.

Outside London! Do you dare?

I have found that many students, especially if they have grown up in London, are sometimes reluctant to consider drama schools in the regions. You must realise that London is awash with actors and it can be quite difficult to get connections with the profession.

In the large, regional metropolitan cities with accredited drama schools there is, without exception, a strong cultural life and, in my experience these schools have found it easier to connect locally with the theatres, film companies and broadcasting organisations than those in London. Liverpool, Bristol, Manchester, Glasgow, Birmingham and Oxford have all well-established drama schools situated in vibrant cultural centres.

Looking at the website

One thing you'll immediately notice is that all the drama schools offer a very similar syllabus. This is hardly surprising as they are all teaching more or less the same thing. But you might like to pause and think about what you're looking at.

Alumni

A word about the alumni who are mentioned by every school in their prospectus or on their website. There are, undoubtedly, some wonderful teachers and inspiring classes in our great catalogue of drama schools, and it is true that some directors have a liking for the kind of actors who come out of a particular school. However it would be wrong to assume that certain actors have become famous simply because of their training. Talent and a good measure of luck go a long way. For example Manchester Met can boast of Sir Anthony Sher, Julie Walters and Bernard Hill. What really set them on the road was being part of the company of actors that Alan Dossor put together at the Liverpool Everyman in the 1970s.

As often happens, one of them got a job at the Everyman and when the chance came up they recommended good people they knew. All credit to Manchester Met, (Manchester Poly as it was then), one of my favourite schools, but they were a group of actors training there more than 40 years ago.

More up to date successful actors, if they have made a name on a TV series, might well have been cast because of their looks.

One or other of the terrible Mitchell twins on Eastenders was cast because he looked enough like the other. None of this is to suggest that any of the actors aren't terrific nor that the schools aren't doing a great job, but the alumni list, both old and new entries, should be thought of as a piece of window dressing.

Apply to a lot of drama schools and don't be out of date

One very odd thing I've discovered is that nearly all auditionees for drama school have a very strange idea of the schools they're applying for. I don't know where these ideas come from, but in my experience they tend to be about 50 years out of date! The kind of thing I'm told is that such and such a drama school only takes tall, public school types, and that another insists that everyone who auditions has to take their clothes off, or that a third school will only take one blonde or redhead girl each year. Whatever might have been the case in the past, the situation now is that all schools are looking for the widest possible cross selection of students.

Associated with these rumours about the selection of students are hugely outdated ideas about the content of the courses at different drama schools. It is perfectly true that 50 or more years ago different schools had very identifiable characteristics. But remember that 50 years ago there were very clear differences between for example, political parties, supermarkets, the high street of different towns and so on. One of the trends of society over the past half century is an increasing similarity, and drama schools have moved in a similar direction.

There is, of course, a difference in emphasis on various aspects of training between the schools, but that's about it. Every course in the country will include physical and vocal technique training, examination of the work of Stanislavski, acting for camera as well as stage, final year public performances of plays and showcases to which agents are invited. Put it this way, who would apply to a drama school which advertised itself by saying it deliberately didn't teach vocal and physical technique or didn't include any reference to Stanislavski, didn't do acting for camera or didn't offer public shows?

To maximise your chance of success you MUST NOT be a snob.

There are 18 drama schools I recommend you investigate. All of them offer outstanding training although there are differences in emphasis.

For example one might offer more classes in dance and movement and another more in vocal technique, but the overall spread of teaching will be very similar in all of them.

The other difference is that some will be better known than others, but take a look at the schools attended by actors in almost any show and you find a wide range including the older more famous and the newer less well known. In terms of getting seen by agents at the end of the course you'll find that good agents realised long ago that the talented actors don't all go to one place and they will be very busy seeing the final shows and showcases of all the drama schools.

Sometimes individual directors and casting directors will establish a relationship with a particular group of drama schools, but you can't take these private preferences into account.

How many schools should I apply to?

Given that all drama schools charge a fee for the privilege of auditioning my answer will be unwelcome I'm afraid. You should apply for as many as possible and spread the choices as widely as possible. There are five central London drama schools which tend to be the names that most people know.

This is because most of them have been around for a long time and have built up a deserved pedigree. Then there are a group of outer London schools, some of which are long established some of which are newer. These have also created a reputation for turning out highly employable actors.

Finally there are the out-of-London schools, which are again a mixture of new and long established places, also with records of great success. You should think of applying for a good mixture of all three types. Apply to at least ten schools and divide your choices into about a third from each category. In my experience the students who are most successful are those who apply to ten or more schools and who don't bias their applications towards one particular group of schools.

I know that this represents a terrific capital outlay, but if you really want to give yourself a fighting chance then you need to start saving now and make all your birthday and Christmas presents the cost of an audition!

All of the drama schools I am about to list offer great teaching and all have produced long lists of successful actors. I've just picked out one or two specifics about each.

Remember very many of the acclaimed teachers work at several drama schools.

The top 18 schools

Academy of Live and Recorded Art or ALRA

ALRA is strongly inclined towards training for screen as much as stage. The schools mentioned below include screen acting but ALRA puts it as equally important as stage acting.

Birmingham School of Acting

This Midlands-based drama school has great proximity to the RSC and has, over the last few years, cultivated good connections with that organisation. It offers a general training in a thriving city where BBC Drama is now based.

Bristol Old Vic

The Bristol Old Vic Theatre School is one of the longest established drama schools in the country offering classical training with a strong emphasis on the vocal aspect of training. They only take a small number of people so a more individualised training is on offer.

Drama Centre London

The Drama Centre emphasises the physical qualities of the actor and has its own specialty called Character Analysis, which is a way of training the transformational aspect of acting.

East 15

East 15 was established to teach actors the style of training used by Joan Littlewood, which includes detailed character work. Mike Leigh and Stephen Daldry are celebrated ex-students.

Guildford School of Acting

GSA became known as a high quality training school because of its music-theatre course and many people still think of it in that way. However it has broadened out and offers a high-class training in straight acting as well as in music-theatre.

Guildhall School of Music and Drama

One of the five central London schools. It gives a well-rounded approach which includes understanding a range of acting philosophies. It is viewed by some as tending toward an elite kind of training establishment. They have a very rigorous entry policy – If you fail to get in after two tries you are not invited to audition again. Students applying have either loved the audition process on offer or loathed it.

Italia Conti

Once a stage school and because of this some students can be sniffy about it, but for many years a fully accredited drama school and it now offers a highly successful and competitive BA Acting course. The training is broad based and aims to produce actors with a flexible attitude. One of the longest established actor training institutions. Do not overlook it.

London Academy Music and Dramatic Arts

Another central London drama school where places are highly sought after. A broad approach to training without an affiliation to one single doctrine. Excellent and newly refurbished facilities.

Liverpool Institute of Performing Arts

(LIPA) is strong on giving its students the tools to enter the profession so they can create their own work. Students get an all around education in both acting skills and the broader opportunities of the profession. Situated in a thriving cultural environment with good local and regional connections.

Manchester Metropolitan University School of Theatre

Like the other schools outside London, students can be much more in touch with the professional opportunities in the region. Manchester also boasts a thriving theatre scene and media connections.

Mountview Academy

At the time of writing Mountview is North London based but has plans to move to new premises South of the river. They are very strong on musical theatre training and very much on the up and up. Look in any West End musical programme and you will see that Mountview is very well represented. Their straight acting course is very good too.

The Royal Academy of Dramatic Art

RADA places strong emphasis on developing skills – voice, physicality, etc. There is less emphasis on transformation and much more on developing the individual's abilities. It is perhaps the most famous drama school in the world established in 1904. While still giving a strong classical training nowadays it works hard to include new plays in its repertoire.

Rose Bruford

Rose Bruford was the first drama school to realise the value of actors who could both act and play musical instruments with their Actor/Musician course. As an old established school it has a successful BA course and has long been recognised as important in actor training.

Royal Central School of Speech and Drama

Central provides the largest number of different courses to be found in any drama school. Consequently there are a lot of students around. The effect of this is many students like being part of a diverse and energetic organization but on the other hand some students prefer a more intimate learning environment which is more commonly found at other schools. That said it offers first class training.

Royal Conservatoire of Scotland

In addition to the standard training, the school has good connections overseas which gives another dimension to the course and has very good facilities.

The Royal Welsh College of Music and Drama

This school has as its USP the creation of a repertory company with the third year actors, so the students get lots of performance experience – a great way to learn the practical application of the skills learnt on the course.

OK, so you've chosen your ten or so schools and are now anxious to get on and prepare your audition speeches. One word of warning here – most people auditioning believe the speech is the only criterion the panel will use to make up its mind about you. Wrong! What counts is a good speech and an overall good impression. A common criticism of students auditioning is that they appear 'over prepared'. By focusing only on the speeches they fail to reveal what all drama school audition panels want to see which is what the real you is like.

Pay attention to what comes next!

Audition speeches

You probably believe that the most important thing in the audition is the speech. However as you will soon discover the first impressions about another person are made almost instantly. These impressions can change and frequently do change, but the audition is a much wider series of impressions which are made by everything you do and say. Remember no one wants to spend three years with a self indulgent, spoilt brat.

Everyone wants to spend three years with someone who has sunshine in their head. That said, the speeches are obviously very important, partly because of what they say about you. Two speeches from very depressed characters might be a reflection of the person giving them. Here are some tips about the speeches themselves.

You must have six speeches prepared before you start out on your audition adventure. - three classical speeches and three contemporary. The classical speeches are the easier ones to find because there are fewer choices!

You'll look at Shakespeare first and discover that once you have narrowed it down to characters who are the right gender, (at the time of writing there are several initiatives to promote cross gender casting, but for the moment I think audition panels prefer gender appropriate characterisations), who are approximately the right age for you, who have a speech about the right length and in some way with whom you can find sympathy, then the field is quite small.

There are several websites you can consult which helpfully list all the monologues in Shakespeare. This is a good place to start, but you obviously must read the whole play, or watch a good film version of it, and then read it to get a proper grip on the character and the situation. A speech from a play you've studied or seen is another useful jumping off point.

What does it mean to 'find a character with whom you can find sympathy'? The guidelines here are pretty broad, but think about yourself.

What is a likely or at least possible casting for you? Forget your childhood dreams and consider, are you more of a tomboy type for whom Joan of Arc (Joan La Pucelle in Shakespeare's Henry VI) or more of a French Princess type from Love's Labours Lost? Are you more likely to be cast as the devilish Iago in Othello or are you a more comedic character like Puck in A Midsummer Night's Dream?

If you are tall and female then Helena in Midsummer Night's Dream would be fine, but not if you're five foot. Most people who are auditioning for drama school are aged between 17 and 23. If you are in the younger part of this age range and look young for your age then a character who talks about his children is out, but a 23 year-old could probably play a character up to the age of 30.

So you have a few ideas of characters you can play and now you have to read the plays more than once to get to grips with the story and the characters.

I suggest you read a synopsis first so you can start to get an idea of the main action and the relationships of the main characters.

Don't be ashamed to read anything that helps you understand the story and the characters – children's stories from Shakespeare, Wikipedia, animated cartoons or some of the very good films which have been made of the great Shakespearean plays. However you introduce yourself to the plays you must then read them.

Now look at what the character you are beginning to like has to say. Do you like the words he has to use? Can you relish the language? Do you see a favourite word or phrase?

Something has to resonate with you and you need to offer that excitement when you do your speeches.

Avoid contemporary speeches which are heavy with detailed sexual descriptions and those with any full-on swearing. You don't want to embarrass the panel or make them squirm with some of the more graphic descriptions of violence in some plays or film speeches.

They will immediately ask the question, 'Why choose that speech when there are all the others to choose from? What kind of applicant is that?' Your choice of speeches is a reflection on you so make sure you choose well.

If you are giving a comic speech don't expect the panel to laugh. Whilst they may well be amused their mind is focusing on a number of different things. If they do laugh it's a bonus but keep the faith. I have known many students who panic on not getting the same reaction they may have got when performing their speech for their friends and rush off and chose a different speech as a result.

Timing! - when should I apply for my auditions?

Most people apply after the New Year. (RADA now charges more for auditions after Christmas in order to try and get more people auditioned earlier.) I don't think it matters too much when you audition. There are wild assumptions and legends abounding about the best time. 'If you apply later on all the places will have gone!' On the other hand people say, 'They wait till later to get the best people!' This is a myth. But I recommend applying so your auditions come between January and March.

Try and arrange for your auditions to be reasonably close to each other so you get on a 'roll' and don't have the long gaps in which you can build up your nerves all over again. However that said you don't want to cram them all into a couple of weeks.

Over a month or six weeks or so would be a realistic time scale.

Of course a lot of the timetable is out of your hands, but again you're not the helpless victim so many candidates think they are in this audition process.

Chapter 6

The audition itself

One caveat – because there are so many people applying for drama schools it's usually the case that the full time staff or the course director won't be there for the first round. It's very often the case that the panel has ex students of the school on it. Very occasionally an older actor whose career is going through a dull patch can seem grumpy and negative as they audition you – young, vital, optimistic. Yes they might be a bit jealous! Just stick to your guns, keep smiling and don't be put off your stride as you do your speeches.

Be prepared for all sorts of things. Other candidates might try and psych you out with boasts about how successful they've been, or with disparaging remarks about your speeches. If you pick up on something like that from one of the other candidates you must isolate yourself and not listen to them.

In some auditions the whole group of applicants do their speeches in front of one another, more often they are private just with the panel. Don't be surprised by either method or by any other method.

The schools aren't trying to catch you out, they've just devised different ways which suit their purposes. Just go with the flow – confidently.

They want you to be good

One thing to always remember about auditions is that the people behind the table are hoping you'll be the answer to their prayers. They are going to see thousands of candidates (quite literally thousands), but they want to discover new and exciting talent, and that might be you!

I know! It certainly doesn't always look like that, and some audition panels might appear bored or indifferent, but that's because they've seen lots of candidates, and despite their best efforts, they can show fatigue in a number of different ways. They can be bored or even seem hostile. But you just rise above it. Whatever it might look like they are really hoping that as you walk into the room you'll be wonderful.

The tricky questions about your speeches or your experience are because they are interested in you, not because they want to catch you out.

Remember the reputation of the drama school depends on the quality of the students. They are thinking of the potential of every candidate and how that person might turn out in three years' time, so they will use a variety of methods to try and get the best. That can include challenging you on the interpretation of your speech or asking you to do it with a radically changed emphasis.

Another subliminal thought in the back of the audition panel's mind, is 'What will it be like to have this person around for three years? Thirty hours a week? Will this candidate be interesting, amusing, intellectually challenging or needy, boring and self centred?'

Are you smiling when you enter the room? How do you stand and sit? Are you creating a good feeling around you? Can you talk with a bit of conviction and authority about the theatre, TV and films you've seen? Are you showing enthusiasm or are you committing the worst sin of all and badmouthing something you saw recently?

NB Accents

Many students think that if they choose a piece in an accent it'll show some of their additional skills. I'd strongly advise against it.

While you are doing your best to sustain your excellent Geordie/Ulster/Welsh/American accent when in fact your natural speaking voice is London, the next person might well have the accent you tried as their birthright. Only use RP or an accent which is yours by upbringing. So, for example, if you were brought up in a household where a parent had a clear Liverpool accent and you have grown up with it, then fair enough, use it in auditions.

If you went to a school in Scotland, but your home accents were RP then you could use a Scottish accent. If it's just an accent you've learnt then give it a miss as far as the speeches are concerned. It won't be convincing enough.

IMPORTANT!

The one thing which comes across from all drama schools is that they want you to be yourself. Simple to say but crucial and very hard to achieve in the few minutes you have, most of which is taken up with those speeches. But this is where it's vital to understand that the speeches are only part of the equation, and it's how you are, your facial expressions, your stance and posture, and so on all count.

You must be as natural as you possibly can be and be yourself not what you think the panel wants you to be. You think they're looking for something 'right for Drama Centre or right for RADA', but in fact they're looking at you to find out what you are like. I know it's impossible in such a short time, but actually all of us give a lot away without knowing it.

Transformation

This is where very many students fall down. You will have spent a long time preparing your speeches, probably with help from a tutor, and you know exactly how it should sound. You know where you want to place the emphasis, which phrases can be more throwaway and which are the heart of the speech. You know the context and have thought carefully about the character, who he/she is and how this speech fits in to the overall development of that character and storyline of the play as a whole.

After so much preparation it is very easy for the speech to become rigid. Your thoughts and emotions about the speech and the character have stagnated. Then suddenly the audition panel ask if your Romeo, rather than being angry at Friar Laurence, who has just told Romeo he is to be banished, could be astonished and jokey. You've never thought this before and while you try and find some differences, it actually comes out strange and forced. This is perhaps the area where candidates for drama schools most often fail.

You need to think about, and practice using your speech in different ways. You must be flexible; after all acting is frequently described as the art of transformation. So you must be prepared to transform!

It's happening in your mind but not as I see it. Actors of long professional experience as well as new, young actors very, very often think they are doing something different whereas to the person watching they are doing more or less the same thing. 'Very good, but can you do the speech with more vitriol? More savagery?' In your mind as you repeat the speech, you are a snarling tiger, Ghengis Khan, a nuclear explosion. On the outside almost nothing has changed. It's all a bit louder perhaps, nothing more.

If you are asked to change the interpretation of your speech do consider the physical changes this might produce. Think of being a different animal and commit yourself wholeheartedly to it. The two reactions you might get from doing your speech in a newly directed way could be: 'Well, there were some little changes there, but nothing very convincing.' Or 'Well, she certainly went for it! Total commitment, even though it wouldn't be right for a whole production'. Commit to it and go for it!

They often get it wrong

In my experience, the traditional drama school audition process is very flawed. The usual format of two speeches, little or no conversation in the first round, followed by a workshop and a short interview in a second or subsequent round is a very subjective and therefore inaccurate way of assessing candidates' true potential. It isn't really any better in the profession except there are usually fewer people so maybe a more realistic appraisal can be made.

We know it's rather flawed because candidates who are rejected by say Guildhall are accepted by say RADA and Central. We know because the same candidate re-applying to the same drama school after a rejection in May is offered a place at the same school six or eight months later. In trying to deal with the huge numbers that apply, the drama schools, if they are honest, often miss out on real talent.

So what does that mean for you? It means you shouldn't be too depressed if you are not lucky. Notice I say 'lucky' because that's what it is, a lot of the time. The great lottery which is called Auditioning!

However you must be realistic as well. Just because the drama schools sometimes get it wrong doesn't mean they always get it wrong. If you have applied several years running and not got a place, then maybe you should turn your artistic imagination in another direction. Be warned! Auditioning and acting can become addictive. As they say, 'Acting? Easy to get into, very difficult to get out of!'

Chapter 7

The obvious questions at a drama school interview

If you get beyond the first day of auditions, and in some cases even on the first day, you will be interviewed. The questions you are likely to be asked are rather predictable, so do think about them and make yourself prepared. Don't learn a series of answers like a script, but think about what you've been doing and what you've seen and so on, so you can talk with fluency and authority.

The ten obvious questions:

Why did you choose that piece?

Why do you want to become an actor?

Why do want to come to this drama school?

What performance have you recently seen that sticks in

your mind?

What will you do if you don't get a place this year?

What are your strengths and weaknesses?

Which actor do you particularly admire?

What performing have you been doing?

What else interests you – hobbies, sports?

What stage are you at with other applications?

You should try and use every opportunity to show you are a broad based, well-informed, committed candidate. They want to know about you.

It isn't a test with right or wrong answers, but you can use every question to tell them more about yourself. Let's go through them one by one to give you an idea of the sort of answers that would be helpful to both you and the panel

Why did you choose that piece?

You will have spent a lot of time searching for your speeches, so you should be able to reply quite easily. The kind of thing to avoid is, 'I felt it was right for me'.

Use the question to say more about yourself and the things you have done. So you might say, 'I saw the play recently, and the character interested me, so I read it carefully and realised I could really sympathise with what the character was talking about'. This way you let them know, for example, that you go to the theatre, and that you read the whole play not just the speech.

Why do you want to become an actor?

Most people find this one very hard to answer. Probably because they want to avoid saying, 'Because I like it when people applaud and admire me'. Fair enough to want to avoid coming across as a complete narcissist, but what can you say? The first obvious thing is that you want to get a proper training, but just saying that is pretty obvious. Ask yourself – training for what?

I suggest you think about the effect seeing a film or watching a play has had on you. So, for example, if you enjoy comedies you might think about the role comedy has in our lives and shape your answer around an idea like, 'I think comedy is an important part of our lives. Seeing the RSC Comedy of Errors I came out of the theatre feeling good, and I'd like to be able to let other people have that feeling'.

Or perhaps you think acting should have some sort of social role, so you might think along the lines of, 'I leant a lot from visits to school by professional actors. In particular a show about bullying was very memorable and had an effect on our year group. I'd like to learn how to do that sort of thing myself'.

Perhaps your only thought is that you'd like to be on stage in a West End musical, with all the glitz that goes with it. In that case think about why those shows are so popular. Generally speaking they let people turn off from the everyday world, and they are undemanding, I mean they are easy to follow (apart from Les Miserables!) and very often have a happy ending. All perfectly commendable things, so you might give an answer along the lines of, 'Lots of musicals are a bit like fairy stories, like Wizard of Oz, they have clear cut characters and difficulties for the hero to overcome, and fairy stories have always been important to society. I want to train to be able to give an audience the excitement that music and dance brings, and the satisfaction that you get from a fairy story or a musical when everything is brought together in a well rounded ending'.

And so on. Do notice that in each answer I've been able to give a little more information about myself, and show that I do go and see actors in action!

A surprisingly large number of people applying for drama school either don't go and see things, or forget to tell us they do. It's very important to know that the candidate is a keen audience member as well as a committed performer.

Why do you want to come to this drama school?

As I said earlier, the huge differences in training that used to exist have shrunk to a large extent. Perhaps there was a time when RADA was very much a posh finishing school and Drama Centre was rightly nicknamed 'Trauma Centre', but today the differences are more in emphasis rather than in basic philosophy.

This is not to say that they're all the same, and you should make yourself aware of their special qualities.

What have you seen recently that sticks in your mind?

As always don't just say, 'I saw Jane Eyre at The National and it was awesome'. Use the question to say extra things about yourself. So you might answer along these lines, 'Well, I go the theatre/cinema every couple of weeks and try and see a very wide range of productions. Jane Eyre at the National was impressive because I hadn't seen a play with live musicians on stage before, and the style of storytelling was very simple but very convincing. I leant a lot from seeing it'

So in that sort of reply you tell the panel that you go regularly, that is to say you are genuinely interested in seeing actors at work, and that you are the sort of person who is able to watch and learn, and that was a good experience for you.

All the time you are trying to say, in a very short time, that you are committed, not just because you say so but because you go and see things as well as doing your own performances.

What will you do if you don't get a place this year?

Opinions differ on the answer to this one. Some people say that it sounds more convincing if you say you're going to get 'life experience' and help build a school in the Third World. I wouldn't argue with that. It's a very laudable thing to do and would undoubtedly help to mature anyone who did it. However I always tell my students that they should stick around and stay in the arts world if not in the acting world. Amazing possibilities can come up.

Among my students forced to take a year off before applying again, one worked with an actors' agency getting very valuable contacts and an inside view of the business, another has been getting professional paid acting jobs and has a pretty good looking portfolio of work, another landed an ongoing character in a major TV series.

All these experiences will be very positive in giving them confidence and an advantage when they come to audition again. If they need to think about drama school again!

What are your strengths and weaknesses?

Candidates often find this a very difficult question to answer because it seems to require a degree of immodesty or is regarded as an invitation to boast. (Incidentally it can also be asked in terms of 'What will you bring to the course?') A good way to answer is to say something along the lines of:

'My teachers at school/friends in my youth theatre/ director of the community play I was in, have said that I'm at ease/confident in, the physical side of acting but need to sharpen up my text work quite a bit.'

Or:

'While I've enjoyed the Shakespeare plays I've seen and been in so far, I know there's a huge amount I need to do to fully understand them and to portray the complexity of the characters. On the other hand the great experience I've had as a singer and musician has given me the basics of a decent voice on which to build.'

Or:

'I've been told I'm a good organiser, so that would be seen as a strength. I'm prompt and well prepared. I know however that my voice needs a lot of work to produce the confident, resonant sound for the classics.'

Or:

'I've done a bit of work on a film and was excited to see professionals at work and was impressed by the speed at which they picked things up. Since then I've worked hard to be prompt and well prepared so I can make the changes that might occur in a rehearsal. On the other hand I know I need to improve my sight reading which is not good at the moment.'

Or:

'People tell me I have a good sense for comedy, which is a nice compliment. But they also tell me that I rely on doing the same or similar things too often, so I need to learn to extend my techniques in comedy and very much in serious plays.'

Given that most candidates for a BA course will be somewhere between 18 and 22 years-old it is a fair bet to say that your voice still needs improvement. Most voices don't settle into maturity until after 20. Unless you've done a lot of sport or dance you are likely to need help in improving yourself physically. Some people have a good ear for accents but most people don't.

As always, assess yourself honestly, and don't invent things which aren't true. The panel want to get a picture of you and how you describe yourself is a part of that impression.

What do you want to get out of this course?

There is no use being overcome with modesty! No-one likes to boast but you can always say something like, 'I was always cast in comic parts at school/youth theatre and seemed to get a good reaction. So I'd like to strengthen my more non comedic, dramatic abilities and I know I must improve my voice'.

Or you might think of saying something like, 'Well I've been told that I can create a convincing character, but I only have the basic ideas of how to do that and I know you are strong on Stanislavski. And I need to improve my stamina.' Or, 'I know I'm strong musically, I play keyboards and sing, but my breathing technique is poor and I find text work a challenge at the moment'.

So each time I am suggesting there is something I can do but as always need to improve and there are other things which I'm poor at and will need a proper training in order to improve.

What actor do you particularly admire?

The obvious answer to this question, which I hear all the time, is either Judi Dench or Jonny Depp or the most recent celebrity actor from that particular drama school! The candidate then says the quality they admire is the variety their hero brings to his work. Not very inspiring.

I suggest you think of an actor who has had an interesting and varied career, but who isn't necessarily in the papers every other day. So think about people like Imelda Staunton, Tilda Swinton, Timothy Spall or Neil Pearson, all actors who have had a long and interesting career.

Again this kind of answer illustrates your knowledge of the profession, which in turn reveals a sort of commitment. However make sure you know about the person you choose. Where did they start and what were the early successes, not just the more recent headline grabbing parts of their biog. And importantly what is it about their career which interests you or coincides with your experience?

Maybe the actor came from the place you were brought up, or was in the same play that you have been in, or you saw them in a theatre or on a live broadcast near where you live. As always it gives more information about you and how you spend your time if you can say, 'I admire Kathryn Hunter, who I saw on tour at my local theatre, because she has played such a rich variety of roles and almost pioneered the idea of cross gender casting. And her training at Le Coq means she brings an extra level of physical and comical skill to her performances. She's in London at the moment playing Cyrano de Bergerac which I hope to see'.

What performing have you been doing?

Don't start with your appearance as a weasel in the local amateur Wind in the Willows when you were four years old!

Pick out two or maximum three recent performances and don't just list them but give some idea of what they meant to you. So for example, 'I was in a youth theatre production of The Crucible in my home town. I was playing Abigail and the thing I learnt for the first time is how much of the time you have to react to what the other actors are doing and how you must keep concentrated for long periods of time. You really need stamina, which is what I hope to build up on a course'.

What else interests you?

They might ask about other interests because, as I said earlier, they are looking for people who have a range of interests as well as being wholly committed to acting. An interest in sports can give evidence of stamina and team playing, while an interest in writing and reading can give evidence of a love of literature. Don't be shy to talk about singing and any musical talent you might have. These all add to the picture of you as an energetic, active and interesting person.

What stage are you at with other applications?

Just be honest and tell them how you're doing. Simple. In fact if there is one key thing to remember about the whole interview part of the audition is to be honest, to be yourself. That's what they really want to know about. Don't try and pull the wool over their eyes!

You will probably only be asked a couple of questions at most (time is of the essence) but remember the answers you give tell them more about the kind of person you are and the kind of actor you want to be. None of the questions have a right or wrong answer. Over my time teaching the foundation course at The Drama Centre I have heard some wonderful well thought-out conspiracy theories about auditions and interviews. Forget all of that. They just want you to talk honestly about yourself. Don't try and second-guess what they want. Prepare yourself by having a think about what your answers might be to the list of questions above. In so doing you will help to focus on who you are and what you really want out of being an actor.

One final and very important point to note about answering questions at your audition is to keep your answers to about 90 seconds maximum. On many occasions I have seen a good answer ruined by random additional comments or observations that are irrelevant and weaken the initial response. So, once you have answered the question have the confidence to stop talking – it's very effective.

Lastly...

A couple of questions you should be asking yourself
What should I wear to the audition?

This is quite easy to sort out. An actor has to inhabit many different roles and versatility is one of the key abilities an actor must display. So for your audition, which might well involve a workshop, you need to be fairly neutral. Shoes will affect the way you move, so be sure you're comfortable in them. Some people want to add bits of costume or props, but I'd advise against it.

They want to see you in contrasting ways and spending time putting on high heels or adjusting a hat adds so little that it's not worth it. Take out any jewellery and piercings. Keep you hair swept back – the panel want to see the subtleties of your performance which they'll miss if you have hair flopping all over your face.

If there's a workshop be sure you wear trainers not clumpy outdoor shoes or boots and certainly not high heels and girls don't wear jewellery! A neutral shirt, blouse or T shirt with loose trousers so you can move about and do some exercises or dancing with freedom is all you need.

What if I don't get in?

Well the first thing to say is that you won't die! So many students behave as if their lives will end if they don't get in. Not true. You'll live to fight another day. I've said what I think you should do above. It's a big disappointment if you don't get a place but if it's the first or second year of drama school auditions then do something constructive and try again. Once you're trying for the third or fourth time you need to think carefully. There are plenty of stories about famous people, like

Judi Dench, who auditioned several times before they were given a place, but…it is the exception not the rule.

Before I hand back to Paul, I'd just like to say one last thing.

You have to understand that the world you're entering is full of the most astonishing opportunities and most heartbreaking disappointments. That's why it's not like working in a shop or an office. Think carefully about it, and if you are disappointed in your application to drama school do remember you will need mental and psychological strength to get through a career in acting.

Often there'll be good surprises, but the sense of incomprehension and the resources needed when it doesn't go your way won't change. That's the actor's life – wonderful, creative and fulfilling, but tremendously demanding of your psychological resources. Stay strong.

Part 3
Relaxation, Rapport, Results!

Ok. Here it is. The bit you've all been waiting for. In this part of the book you will learn a whole host of techniques to reduce your audition anxiety and enhance your ability to impress.

Chapter 8

Waiting for an audition

What is it like having to wait for an audition? I don't mean the long wait that lasts days, weeks, sometimes months. The one where you are sitting at home, rocking yourself back and forth while you stare wide eyed at the phone shouting 'Ring you Bastard' every ten minutes. No, I mean the one when you are quite literally sitting in a reception room waiting for your turn to go in and give of your best. It can be quite a difficult ten minutes or so (particularly if you really *have* had to wait months for the opportunity).

I've seen it time without number. An actor will walk into the reception room of an audition with great brio, look around to survey the room, walk to the desk and announce himself with a grounded sense of assurance, 'John Smith, to see Susie Figiss. I believe I'm booked in for 10.45?' He will give the person behind the desk a gracious smile and move over to find a seat upon which he will sit with an upright and open posture. Perfect. If nothing else, we actors at least know how to make an entrance.

Not only have I seen it time without number but I have been that brave actor on countless occasions myself. I've walked in and projected confidence and professionalism in the first minute of my arrival. There's no doubt about it, the receptionist thinks I'm fantastic.

But then, if we're not careful, something strange can start to happen. As we sit and wait it is very probable that our confidence will start to ebb away from us. As we look around at the others who are waiting we can very quickly talk ourself out of the job. 'I recognise him. God, he literally never stops working' and with that thought we shrink a little in our chair. Then, 'Christ, that bloke's tall. Hang on they're all tall! Why am I the only short arse here?' - more negative thinking as our shoulders drop, we fold our arms tightly across our chest and we start to stare at the floor.

The likelihood is that your appointed time will pass because they are running behind giving you only more time to sit and ponder the negatives. 'Why is everybody here so much better looking than me? I shouldn't be here. What a total waste of bloody time. I never get a job with this casting director anyway...I don't know why I bother coming to these things, I'm never good with out proper preparation and they only ever give you three minutes with the script...' and so it goes on until, by the time you are called in; you are more tightly wound than a clock spring.

And what vision awaits the casting director as she calls you through? A hunched over, poe-faced ball of nervousness and anxiety. *This* is the first impression that *really* matters and you just blew it!

There is a touch of 'chicken and egg' about what I'm going to describe to you. Negative thoughts will create a negative posture and negative posture will feed our negative thoughts – or equally, negative posture will create negative thoughts which will create more negative posture... So how do we break the cycle? And is this even true in the first place?

What I just described to you is your fight or flight system kicking in and preparing your mind and body for your audition. The problem is, as described; it's not actually that helpful. Along with everything I have just mentioned you can throw in butterflies, rapid heartbeat, shallow breathing and lack of focus into the pot of unwelcome fight or flight responses.

But responses to what?

The fight or flight system is the oldest part of the brain. Its sole purpose is to keep you alive so why does it jump into action so resolutely when you're only going up for a biscuit commercial?

The fight or flight system has been evolving for over half a billion years and it will leap to your defence whenever it identifies a situation where it cannot tell the outcome. In the old days this might have meant being chased by a sabre toothed tiger. In a modern context this, rather frustratingly, includes job interviews and auditions.

Think about it for a moment. When you go for a job you simply do not know how it will go. Will the panel be receptive? You may not be on form that day and your choices might be a bit crappy. If a song is involved the pianist might not be a very good accompanist, you might forget the lyrics, you may miss the top A. The possibilities of what might go wrong are endless and that is why our fight or flight goes into action. And it does so in two distinct ways – physically and mentally.

Physically you will lower your centre of gravity to be ready to run. At the same time you will also be making yourself smaller, hunching your shoulders, lowering your forehead, pulling in at the tummy. This is to make you less visible – hoping that the sabre toothed tiger might not see you in the first place. Your heart rate will quicken and your breathing rate will speed up to oxygenate your blood. At the same time the blood will travel from your viscera (giving you butterflies in your tummy) to your arms and legs filling them with highly oxygen enriched blood, enabling you to either fight like hell or run for the hills. This is all fantastic if we are faced with a starving quadruped that is placed higher up the food chain than ourselves – a warm and cuddly casting director should not illicit this response but she does.

Mentally two things happen. Firstly, you will be placed on

high alert to seek out possible threat scenarios like, forgetting your words, not hitting the high note etc. The second thing that happens is that the higher thinking part of the brain, the neo cortex, shuts down. Yep, that's right. Rational thought takes a back seat. Why? Because rational thought takes time. If it was a sabre toothed tiger running toward you and you ran through all your options of escape before you had come down to a decision, however well judged, you'd already be halfway down the tiger's throat. The problem with all of this is that it puts you in a very negative place for your interview. But the great thing is we are about to change that right now and forever!

Exercise:

- I want you to go and get a chair with a straight back.
- Now place yourself on the chair in a reasonably neutral physical state for the count of ten.
- Monitor how you are feeling during this time.
- When you hit the number ten I want you to slouch in your chair.

What differences do you notice in the way it changes the way you feel? I guarantee you will suddenly be feeling sluggish, switched off, tired and de-energised. It is extraordinary how immediately ones feelings change due to the way we are holding ourselves.

The science of embodied cognition basically claims that the state of the human body DICTATES the state of the human mind. In other words, what you do, you'll feel. How amazing then to know that, in just the same way as you created a negative feeling just now, you can make yourself feel positive and energised within an instant just by changing your posture!

Before I show you how to achieve this I want you to go into the slouched position again and this time I want you to take a deep nourishing breath.

You can't do it can you? That is because the slouched, hunched over position you have adopted is a fight or flight position, which will encourage you to shallow breathe so that you can oxygenate your blood. While doing this you are going into the low grade fight or flight responses. See what I mean about chicken and egg?

Another fight or flight response is for the sinews in our muscles to stiffen so that we are literally hardened for the ordeal ahead of us.

A second quick exercise:

- Sitting on your chair cross your arms and put a small amount of tension through the muscles.
- Now try and take another deep breath.

You will find it impossible. Even a small amount of tension in the arms, legs or back will result in your ability to breath efficiently being extremely hampered. This is another way of your body forcing you to shallow breath. The difficulty is that we need good belts of oxygen to remain calm and focussed. With all this in mind I think you will agree that how we sit as we wait for our audition is vital.

What I am about to describe, as with most of the techniques in this book will confound you in its simplicity. It is easy to master and its effect is instantaneous. It is a highly effective seated position that I call the 'Ready, Steady, Go'. I use it before each audition or interview I go for because it puts me in the right physical and emotional state. It encourages confidence and a 'can do' frame of mind. It also energises whilst keeping your fight or flight responses in check.

Ready, Steady, Go!

- Perch your bum on the front of the chair
- Straighten your back
- Open up your shoulders
- Hold your head up
- Place your right foot in front of you
- Place your left foot behind your right
- Rest your hands together gently in your lap

This seated position will immediately make you feel quite literally ready, steady and good to go!

In this position you will notice how easy it is to take a deep, nourishing, calming breath that will feed the brain and keep you focussed. All the fight or flight responses will be held in check because you are breathing well and sitting up straight. You will find as well that, seated in 'ready, steady, go'; you will feel a gentle sense of confidence. The negative voices in your head will be quietened. With your head up you avoid staring at the floor, which will stop you internalising in the negative, and keep you consciously 'in the room'.

The other great benefit of 'ready, steady, go' is that you will be putting out the most incredibly positive vibe. When the casting director pops her head out to collect you her first impression of you will look energised and self-assured. This is hugely important because the casting director has a great deal of influence in the choosing of who gets what part. By striking a great first impression from the first moment she sees you she is far more likely to be on your side when the post casting discussions are held.

Furthermore, when you walk into the room you will be carrying that confidence with you all the way. Your thinking processes will be positive, sharp and relaxed helping you to tap into your creative processes aiding you to give a spontaneous and truly 'in the moment' audition. All this from just sitting up straight!

Chapter 9

The value of a great first impression

Surely what happens *before* you go into the audition has no relevance? The true value of a good audition can only be based on how we perform during the interview itself? These are fair assumptions but I assure you they are wrong.

How we prepare our mind and body for the audition experience is of paramount importance. Let's look at the value of creating a great first impression. As already described in the previous chapter, if we allow our fight or flight system to get the upper hand we are going to go into the room full of nerves and negativity. Not only that we will be seen to be nervous or ill at ease at best. And our feelings are contagious. They spread like wildfire so far better to spread feelings of calm, focussed confidence.

By using 'ready, steady, go', as you wait to go in, for instance you will already have insured that you are feeling confident and looking confident. Here's a quick question. When do directors make up their mind about who they want to use?

Have you ever heard this expression before? 'I knew they were the right person for the job the second they walked into the room'.

Am I being serious? Can people really clinch an audition the second they walk in? Before they have said a word? I think so. Don't get me wrong, a strong and positive first impression has to be backed up with ability, insight and a solid performance but as I have already said, there will be many people auditioning who will provide those things. You will stand out from the crowd by allowing the audition panel see you for who you are at your most assured, relaxed and natural the very instant they clap eyes on you. Its potency cannot be overestimated.

Also, thinking bigger picture, while a good first impression does not guarantee getting the job on the day, it will greatly enhance the prospect of a director or casting director bringing you in for another project in the future. This all goes back to my assertion that a good audition is never wasted. The business is littered with stories of people who may not have got the job on the day but were brought back for another project.

The best example of this I can give is Martin Sheen who auditioned for the part of Michael Corleone in The Godfather. He auditioned well but the part went to Al Pacino. However, all was not lost for Martin who was later cast by Francis Ford Coppola in his legendary war epic, 'Apocalypse Now'.

How long does it take to make first impression?

This is a question I ask at all my audition workshops. The answers I'm given range from half a minute to half a second. In his book 'Blink' self proclaimed 'social adventurer' Malcolm Gladwell suggest that we have just a fiftieth of a second! That's quicker than it takes to blink – hence the title of his book. Ponder that one for a while and then consider this: If you make a bad first impression it can take a person up to four years to change their minds about you.

Now do you see the power of a first impression? Make a good one and you're on track to create the basis of a long lasting business relationship, blow it and it's adios amigo!

The good news is that creating a good first impression can be done without saying a word, in fact, there is no other way of doing it. If Malcolm Gladwell is right then there is nothing you can say in a fiftieth of a second that will help or hinder matters either way.

It begs the question how do we communicate in the first place. If it's not with words where does communication start and what can we do to enhance our non verbal messaging?

It breaks down like this:

Words	7%
Tone of voice	38%
Body language	55%

But perhaps it is better viewed like this:

Body language	55%
Tone of voice	38%
Words	7%

Looking at this simple set of percentages where does the power lie in the way we communicate? Well, of course it is in the body language. Then it is the noise we make- how we say what we say. Finally the words we use. Fascinating isn't it? What we actually *say* carries the least power and has the least impact.

For a potential employer to want to have you in their production they are going to want to trust that you will bring not just your talent but your goodwill and a positive attitude to the working environment. But, here's the thing; we rarely start to trust someone based on what they say but almost always on the way we see them behave. We always believe what we see over what we hear, so having an understanding of how to project a persuasive and positive message through our body language is a sure-fire way to create instant and lasting rapport.

With the help of the simple 'Ready, Steady, Go' sitting posture you will have already upped your ability to project confidence to others while instilling confidence in yourself. I now want to add one more simple technique to 'Ready, Steady, Go' that will enhance that confidence and, at the same time, put people at ease in your company so that they really look forward to your audition.

Let's remind ourselves of the basic 'Ready, Steady, Go'
- Perch your bum on the front of the chair
- Straighten your back
- Open up your shoulders
- Hold your head up
- Place your right foot in front of you
- Place your left foot behind your right
- Rest your hands together gently in your lap

Now I want you to add one more ingredient:
- Smile

It couldn't be simpler could it? By choosing to smile you will set off a series of reactions within your own physiology and your immediate environment and they are all positive!

Am I teaching my mother to suck eggs? Don't we all smile when we are greeted by someone? Probably but I'm not just talking about smiling when you see the person who is going to escort you into the audition, I am talking about smiling to yourself as you *wait* for that person. And not smiling like there is something wrong with you, like a Cheshire cat or worse, Tony Blair. For the most part I am suggesting that you have a gentle smile *behind* the eyes and, as the time draws near for your appointment, letting it spread very gently to your lips.

The reasons why a gentle smile will put you in a better place for your audition are manifold. The first one being that by holding a smile your endocrine system will give you a burst of endorphins. These will give you an emotional lift and put you in a more positive and upbeat frame of mind. In short, it will make you feel happy!

How sickening! How horribly schmaltzy, I know! But it is none the less true that if you put a smile on your face you will have a smile in your heart. It is the most fantastic antidote to your fight or flight system's annoying habit of coming at you with negative thoughts. Negative thoughts lead to negative posture that will lead to more negative thoughts. It is literally impossible to feel in a negative space if you put a smile on your face and hold it there for thirty seconds. Remember our new friend, embodied cognition? What you do – you will feel.

Along with the endorphins comes a sense of calmness. When

was the last time you were happy but uptight? The two are pretty much mutually exclusive. By choosing to smile you are making the conscious decision to take control of your feelings and put them in the positive. This is all great but how will a smile have an immediate affect on your immediate environment?

Mirror, mirror on the wall

Part of the reason why human beings have been around for so long is that they work in groups. We are sociable animals and for the most part we work for the benefit of the tribe. For that to work we need consensus on what is the right thing to do, the right place to go and who are the right people to hang out with or, indeed, employ. However, to reach consensus we have to follow a leader and thus all humans are hard wired to follow the leader. But who is the leader?

This next bit might surprise you.

When you go into an audition YOU become the leader. You are the initiator and the person everybody on the panel will be taking their cues from. The pack will be following you! It is incredibly empowering to know that the emotional state that you project will be reflected back to you immediately.

Each human being has a part of the brain called the Mirroring Neuron. One of its functions is to help encourage empathy by helping us to understand the actions and intentions of other people by copying them – by putting ourselves in the same physical and emotional state to achieve harmony and understanding. It is a mechanism that very quickly puts us on the same wavelength. And again, I'm tempted to ask what wavelength do you want to share with your interviewer? One where you both share a sense of tension, where you are both on edge? Of course not! Where would be the sense in that?

Taking the deliberate choice to enter a room with a good positive posture and a warm but gentle smile will, ninety nine times out of a hundred, help you to open the batting with the confidence of knowing that you are leading the herd to a positive and open frame of mind.

Theatre director and actor Paul Clayton once said something to me about holding auditions that I've never forgotten. 'Half the time you are baby-sitting people who can't handle the stress of the situation. You end up spending a huge amount of time just helping them to let go of their nerves so that they can sing their song or read without their anxieties getting in the way. I always get really excited when an actor walks in and is relaxed because if they are relaxed I can relax and straight away we can get on with the audition. It's immediately more impressive'.

So, to recap -

A smile affects your immediate environment because it will put those around you at ease. If you smile, their mirroring neuron will kick in and they will smile too. They in turn will get a little burst of happy-making endorphins too and know deep in their psyche that they can relax and crack on with the audition with no element of hand holding. You will find yourself on the same wavelength and their defences will drop, paving the way to an open and constructive interview.

And all this before you've said a single word!

It's a point worth making that people (particularly the techno natives) are falling out of the habit of smiling. Go into any shop and, most of the time you will find that the person serving you has their face buried into the screen on the till, will give you little or no eye contact and will not smile.

This type of exchange is called 'transactional'. There is technically nothing wrong with the service you are being given except that it lacks warmth and a sense of humanity.

It is something you should fight against with all your might.

We are not here to be merely functional. Our personality must shine through all our interactions and the simplest way of allowing that to happen is to smile.

There are many things I find difficult and frustrating and even embarrassing about being me but the one thing I love about being Paul Ryan is the fact that the world smiles at me. Why? Because I smile at it and it genuinely makes the world a happier place for me to be in.

Please use this simple but highly powerful piece of body language to draw people close to you not just in an audition scenario but in everyday life. I cannot over stress its potency.

Chapter 10

How best to 'press the flesh'

So far so good.

'Ready, steady, go' has put you in a great place as you wait for your audition. As the time draws near you move the smile from behind your eyes to broaden your lips so that when you are greeted by the casting director they get a fantastic first impression of you as relaxed, open and in control. On seeing you they break into a smile helping you to feel further relaxed. Keeping all this in place you enter the audition room and are introduced to the person/people you are auditioning for. You have fantastic posture and a warm smile as you approach them to shake their hand.

Shake their hand? Is this normal? Is this standard? Does it always happen every time?

Yes, you will often be offered a handshake. Yes, it is fairly common practice. No it doesn't happen every time but *most* of the time. For that reason it is of critical importance that you use this, seemingly innocuous, social grace as a golden opportunity to enhance your positive first impression to a whole other level.

I wonder if you have ever given any thought to the way you shake hands with somebody or, indeed why you do it in the first place? Is it merely a social nicety or are there other things going on in the more primal level as we make this all important first physical contact? It is of course the latter and when we have an understanding of what a handshake signifies and what can be communicated by it we will gain further mastery of our rapport building skills.

Done well, a handshake will make people trust you immediately, done badly and you can send out non-verbal messages that will make people dismissive, suspicious or, worse still, downright hostile towards you.

Why do it in the first place?

In a way you are better to ask why *did* we do it in the first place.

Guess what? It all started back in the days when we were cavemen. Didn't everything?!

Let's go back in time a couple of hundred thousand years. What would you do if you came upon a wandering homo sapien on your travels over the savannah who wasn't one of your tribe? The easiest thing to do would be to just run or hide but remember we are sociable animals. We like the company of others now as in prehistoric times, and there is real strength in numbers, so there would be good sense in forming alliances with him – as long as you can establish that he is not going to kill you.

But how would you ascertain that he wasn't going to cause you harm?

The first thing you would do is view them from afar, watch

their body language and how they move to judge if they were a possible friend or enemy. If, when they saw you, they held their ground and gave you sustained eye contact you might be encouraged to move closer and form a possible alignment.

The next thing to do is to slowly move closer to make sure they are not going to hit out at you when you get to within striking distance. As both cavemen cross into each other's personal territory without incident they will move out a hand to gently touch their possible new 'friend' around the abdomen or shoulder to further investigate their intent as being passive or aggressive.

At this point each cave man can see that the other's hand does not contain any stone, cudgel or weapon of any kind that could be used to attack. When this empty handed touch has been accepted and neither party has struck out they can both relax secure in the knowledge that no harm will come to them and that they are safe in each other's company to forage, hunt and gather together.

That was then, this is now...

Over the millennia this cautious ceremony has slowly turned into the handshake we have come to know but its primal purpose is exactly the same – a way of gauging whether a new person is a friend or foe. The modern handshake remains a way to show that we carry no weapons and mean no harm. Take all religious connotations out of the equation and we are literally offering the sign of peace. We are hoping to gain the trust of the person we are touching to show we are at one with them and wish to further our relationship.

But we do not all shake hands in the same way and some of us do it better than others. For example, when I deliver my audition master class I will shake the hands of three people one after the other and ask them how I came across. One will say I gave them the creeps, the next; that I seemed arrogant and the last will comment on how I seemed controlling. The same me, three different handshakes and three completely different emotional responses from the people with whom I shook hands with.

My point is that the way you shake someone's hand has a huge and immediate impact on the way that person will feel about you.

Before we look at your handshaking modus operandi, let's think about the handshakes you may have come across in the past and how they have an immediate impact on your feelings towards that person whose hand you are in the process of shaking.

The wet fish

You know what I am about to describe.

You put out your hand and the person you are introducing yourself to offers you a limp, almost lifeless hand accompanied by a rather gutless shaking motion that more resembles them laying their hand in a bowl of lukewarm soup touching only with the fingers and applying hardly any grip at all. Matters are made worse by a shifty stare and an unconvincing smile. Yes, you have just experienced the 'wet fish' handshake.

We have all experienced this and even as you read my description you can probably feel your skin starting to crawl at the very thought of it. When I demonstrate this to people in my audition skills master class they will often wince, occasionally pull their hand out of mine and every now and then actually have a wee shiver!

Usually when I ask a class of people if they have experienced this most unsettling of handshakes everybody put their hand up. Conversely, when I ask how many actually *give* this handshake no hands go up! Which is only amusing because the maths on that don't stack up.

Why do we find the wet fish handshake so horrible? What is it that makes it so very unsettling?

It is because we are not connecting palms as effectively as we should.

Remember we have to show that we have no weapons or our fight or flight system will send out signals that we are not on safe ground with this person. The light grip implies a lack of strength, therefore you offer little by way of being a good hunting partner and the poor eye contact implies that you are hiding something.

The vice

This is the one where the person takes your hand and crushes the bones of your knuckles together and yanks your arm like they are working a rusty one-armed bandit. This may be accompanied by a hard stare and no smile.

Do you recognize this handshake? Of course, it's very common. When you receive a handshake like this how does it make you feel? Welcomed? At ease? As though the person holds you in high esteem? Of course not! It is a horribly aggressive way of shaking someone's hand. This handshake is all about power play. It is very common in the military and a lot of corporate movers and shakers use this one to impose their authority over their subordinates. It tends to be a mostly male way of handshaking and I think some of the people that use it consider that this is the 'right way' to give a good 'man's handshake'. Yes, we like it firm but not painful.

The covering stab

The handshake where the person will swoop a rigid hand towards you with their palm facing the ground (a bit like a karate chop). When you take their hand they will usually give one short tug on the arm and release you very quickly.

When I've demonstrated this handshake on people they say that it feels very controlling and harsh.

The empty cup cake

This is a subtle cross between the covering stab and the wet fish.

While there is a reasonably strong grip the palm of the hand is deliberately held away and has the unnerving impression of being offered something that isn't actually there! In general responses to this handshake are that it just feels weird.

So here's my question, when you shake hands how do you think you come across?

Ask yourself if you are guilty of using any of these handshakes. If you are you're doing yourself no favours when it comes to making that all-important first impression. Any good work you have done with your positive posture and non-verbal communications will be undone in a moment and you will have given yourself a new set of blockers to overcome before you strike rapport once more.

Now is the time to take a moment to consider how you shake somebody's hand and what affect you are hoping to achieve by doing so.

As actors we like to think of ourselves as brilliant communicators above reproach for how we interact with those around us. I would say, in general, in comparison to other professions this is probably true but we are not perfect and can all benefit from learning the odd new trick here and there. So as you consider the way you shake people's hands be honest, is there room for improvement?

I will now teach you the handshake that will make people like you, trust you and be far more open to employing you. As with most, if not all of the techniques in this book, I would encourage you to use it in your everyday life as well as with specific regard to the audition environment.

The best handshake in the world

There are two parts to this handshake if you are to get the maximum rapport building currency from it. The first part is easy and highly effective. The second part will take time to master before it feels comfortable for both you and the recipient but it really is worth taking this time because when you have both parts mastered you will be like a body language Ninja. This handshake will bring people's natural defences down and make them open to the power of your personality and encourage that all-important trust I spoke of earlier.

The open handshake – part 1

The first thing to say is for this to work you must initiate the handshake. In doing this you become the leader and the other person will follow you.

Hold out your hand and imagine that you are holding a dinner plate on it at an angle of about 65 degrees. Now look down at that hand. What do you see?

An open palm

It's as simple as that! In body language terms an open palm is equal to honesty. We are showing that there is no weapon or cudgel in our hand.

Because you have led this physical exchange the other

person (let's call them the correspondent for the purposes of this exercise) will follow your lead by putting their hand over yours as they go to shake it. When you take their hand give it a firm squeeze as you offer them good eye contact and a gentle smile.

You are literally giving them the upper hand. In a way you are encouraging them to perform the covering stab on you but what is fantastic about this is that, unlike the covering stab, you will be raising their status while losing none of your own.

The fight or flight system in the correspondent will recognise all the body language signals you are putting out and because of what you are physically demonstrating they will feel instantly put at ease. No warning lights will go off about you being a possible threat and you will be identified as a friend. We all feel positively towards our friends but more importantly we want the best for them. So if the hand you are shaking is the hand of a director you will effectively be getting them on side straight away.

To further place yourself in correspondent's circle of trust you must use the second part of this highly powerful set of body language signals.

The open handshake – part 2

So...the correspondent has placed his hand in your upturned palm. You have given it a firm (but not too firm) squeeze, gently shaking rocking the arm up and down while holding eye contact and smiling.

Now...

Take two short steps in towards the correspondent drawing yourself to them allowing the fingers of their hand to move into the area of your stomach. (When you get really good at this you can actually rest the knuckles of their fingers against your abdomen!)

Reading this last paragraph back I can see how you might think I've suddenly gone a bit sleazy. I promise I haven't. It's true that when you first practice this part of the handshake you will probably be accused of space invading. Also, it is easy to make the mistake of yanking the correspondent's hand into your stomach so violently that you dislocate their shoulder.

Like I said, it will take practice but stick with it because when you have learnt to do this with élan you will cause no offence at all but silently strengthen the non-verbal message that you are a person to be trusted. It sounds like a wildly over exaggerated claim doesn't it? Let me explain how it works.

In doing as described you are drawing the attention of your correspondent's fight or flight system to the fact that you are moving their hand in close proximity to the soft, unprotected part of your body where a great deal of your vital organs reside. By doing this the message that will be picked up is 'All my defences are down, I trust you completely not to cause me harm'.

Within a 50th of a second the defences of your correspondent will come tumbling down leaving them open to your influence and ready to see whatever good stuff you have to offer – be it a great reading, a fantastic song or an amazing dance – with an attitude which is far more receptive, supportive and on side because of all the signals you sent out with your handshake.

There is one thing that I would urge you to avoid when shaking the hand of business people you are meeting for the first time.

Do not get your left hand involved in any way!

A left hand should only be introduced when you are shaking the hand of people you know. It is a signal of intimacy that is inappropriate on a first meeting.

To be honest, even when you know someone you can still get it wrong. Many people think that by putting their left hand over your right hand they are showing warmth and support. They might think this but, in fact, the non-verbal message they are sending out is the opposite. They are signalling their perceived control over you.

Just as a matter of interest, if you want to show warmth and support take your left hand and place it *under* the right hand of your correspondent. You will see this handshake a lot at funerals – and weddings if people think the bride is marrying the wrong bloke!

Once again, as with the previous techniques, I would urge you to start using this handshake from now on. Get used to using it on non-showbiz folk so that when the time comes to utilize its power in a professional setting it will happen naturally and without awkwardness.

One last thing on this subject – I use this handshake all the time and with whomever I meet. When I run a workshop I will always introduce myself using the open handshake (parts one and two) making sure I place any correspondent's hand physically against my tummy. Later, when we discuss handshakes people insist that part two is invasive and impossible to achieve without being perceived as weird. I then point out I used that method when I greeted them earlier and no one felt I invaded their space and made no one feel uncomfortable.

Also, the open handshake takes the stress out of shaking hands because it is so very pacific. And if I feel at peace when I am offering my hand people will feel at peace when they take it – harmony is assured, rapport is struck. You have put yourself on the same wavelength within a moment and identified your self as trustworthy. What's not to like?!

Chapter 11

In your own time...

So you've made a confident start to your audition and you are secure in knowing that the first 50th of a second went brilliantly. Congratulations you are well on your way. Once the fight or flight of your interviewer has subconsciously identified you as a friend their pre frontal cortex (the higher thinking part of the brain) will then start making conscious decisions that will fall in line to back up the signals of their fight or flight response to you. Basically, they will begin to warm to you.

Now, if you are lucky you will be invited to take a seat. What physical posture will you utilise to send out signals of confidence while keeping your breathing efficient and help you to focus?

Yes, 'ready, steady, go' of course!

This is equally powerful in the interview part of your audition as it is while you are waiting to go in. Your upright posture will make you feel confident and you will be perceived as confident. A light cross of the legs is allowable (not to tightly held and never intertwined) your hands are placed together and resting gently on your lap. This is a light cross that doesn't stop you from being able to breath well. You have a gentle smile, which is both making you feel relaxed and sending out a positive piece of body language that is being reflected back at you. So far, so good.

But what if...

You are not invited to sit!

What if, as often happens in singing auditions and adverts castings you are asked to stand on a mark on the floor? In the pre-epiphany part of my career I always found this one of the most awkward parts of an audition– having to stand still in front of an interview panel while they ask you questions or as you have to wait for the introduction of your song to be played before you can get on with singing it.

This brief part of the audition can feel like an eternity of discomfort.

All of a sudden you are up there, fully exposed and alone. It is at this moment that your fight or flight will have a knee jerk response and kick in once more. Arms may fold, chest may sink, and your head may droop to on side. You might even shuffle around for no apparent reason, realise that you are shuffling but *still keep shuffling!*

The list of nervous habits ticks and twitches may continue. You may fiddle with your fingers or have one arm dropped to one side while your right hand grips your left elbow.

Your shoulders may become tense and your facial expressions may become rigid. Despite yourself you might start speaking too rapidly, your vocal tone may be too high or too low. It could be that you can't help stumbling on your words or you lose your train of thought. All that I have just described are things that I have found myself doing as I stand under the watchful eye of a director. It is what is known in body language terms as emotional leakage.

The difficulty with all these strange and sudden manifestations of nerves is that you will be sending out an incongruent message to your interviewer. If you sing well but you look nervous the person holding the interview will suffer something called 'emotional dissonance'. In short they won't know what to think about you. But as people will always believe what they see over what they hear, ultimately if you look nervous they will perceive you as nervous which, despite how well you sing will unnerve them.

Well not any more. I am going to take you through a list of six things that will always make you feel calm, centred and focused. These six things when used together will also stop all the ticks and twitches associated with emotional leakage insuring that you will always come across as open and in control; unflustered and ready to go.

Yes, I am going to teach you the six parts of my positive posture package – good for everyday life and great for every audition you ever go for. If you use this combination of postures I guarantee that you will feel calm focused and assured in every audition you ever go for. Exciting isn't it?

I will teach you where to place your feet, head, chest, back side and mouth. On top of all that I will answer the question that has plagued actors throughout the ages. What to do with your hands!

Before we go through this remarkably simple but highly effective set of postures I think it will be of value to remind ourselves that as you change your posture you will be changing the way you feel. Two things are at play here, our old friend embodied cognition and a new area of brain science that is being researched as we speak.

Pro-prioceptive psychology is another force at work that helps us to reverse-engineer our feelings. Just as when we put on a smile we make ourselves actually feel happy when we are not, by altering our bodily posture we can move from feeling nervous and unsure to confident and assured.

Happy Feet

During the times when I have sat on the audition panel for various productions I have seen people do the weirdest thing with their feet. I call them unhappy feet.

I have seen them placed wide apart, pushed tightly together, I have seen one foot placed behind the other and then seen the person rocking back and forth for no apparent reason. I have seen people rest their weight on one foot while resting on the heel of the other and waggling their toes. A common unhappy feet position is to stand with your legs tightly crossed sometimes making the person look like a human corkscrew! The list goes on.

Try some of these unhappy feet positions. Do any of them make you feel centred, balanced, in control or in a state of equilibrium? Of course they don't so why do we find ourselves doing them?

It's such a funny notion but we need to rehearse how we stand.

Do this now:

As you stand I want you to place your feet directly underneath your hips distributing the weight evenly between them both. How does that feel? Good eh? And isn't it simple?

By doing this you will feel instantly more centred and in control. I call these happy feet!

Now put your feet very close together. This is a position born of stress. Ironically it will make you feel more nervous than you otherwise would. Try a couple of the other unhappy feet positions again. They only serve to make you look and feel uncomfortable.

Practice standing with your feet directly underneath your hips as often as you can. Get used to doing this. It will give you a real sense of being grounded. It is a wonderful thought that if you stand well upon the earth you have a whole planet supporting you.

Head

In a situation that is stressful your head drops as a fight or flight response. This encourages shallow breathing and will lead to loss of focus. In dropping your head you are lowering your centre of gravity to enable a quick getaway while covering your neck from attack. Now, bad as some auditions can be your life will never be in danger so...

Do this now:

Stand with happy feet and imagine that you have a string running up through your pelvic floor, through your abdomen, up the trunk of your body and out through the top of your head. Now imagine at the top of that piece of string is a balloon and imagine that the balloon is slowly being filled with helium. As it fills it lifts your head into an upright position until you reach your full height.

It is imperative that you imagine the string coming out of the centre of the top of your head. Not the top of your forehead or the crown but the apex of your cranium. In this way when you fill your balloon you will raise your head upright and not at a strange or unhelpful angle.

In doing this you will feel more confident. Your breathing apparatus will be straightened out so that your breathing will be efficient and unlabored. With this upright stance the air you pull into your body will go down to the bottom of your lungs keeping you calm focused and properly oxygenated.

One of the greatest benefits of standing up straight is that it will make you feel energized and present. Let's try it in reverse.

Do this now:

Stand with happy feet and pull your string so that you are fully upright. Now slouch.

The difference in feeling is both remarkable and immediate isn't it! When you slouch you can feel your energy vanish to be replaced with a sense of lethargy and a lack of enthusiasm. Use your happy feet and string and instantly you feel grounded, focused and confident.

How we hold our heads is very telling to the attitude we have in life. A pessimist will walk around with his head down, an optimist will have his head up.

The pessimist will be staring at the ground, cut off from other people and lost in his own thoughts while the optimist will have his eyes set firmly on the world before him making him live in the moment and more easily affected by the positive stimulus of other people.

What is incredible to me is that this advice for making yourself feel more cheerful and confident is part of our everyday parlance.

'Chin up'.

Chest

When we feel nervous or under threat we will allow our chest to sink, which in turn will make our shoulders drop. Once again this will affect our breathing and will cause us to feel a lack of confidence. Not only that but anyone viewing your body language will interpret these signals as timid and lacking in confidence.

When you use happy feet and your string you will be going a long way to correcting this but let's look at the chest in isolation. First I want you to allow your chest and shoulders to sink in the way previously described. As you do you will feel your energy becoming sapped and a subtle lack of confidence creep over you.

Now lift your chest up and as you do push your shoulders back. Only go to a place that is comfortable and when you reach that point take a moment to sense how different it makes you feel.

I'm aware that I sound a bit like a sergeant major in the

army. Chest out! Shoulders back! But maybe it is a good idea to ask why the military want their men to stand in this fashion? Because it makes them a force to be reckoned with. When we see those who are our first line of defence we must have confidence in them and standing in this manner will ensure that they come across as strong and capable – just as you will be when you go into your audition. And here's where a little bit of pro-prioceptive psychology works in your favour. By standing in an upright and confident position you will feel upright and confident. Simple!

Rump

To add greater strength to your posture I want you to pretend that you have a lemon between your butt cheeks and give it a good squeeze! I know it sounds a bit exotic but go with it. It is a technique that I believe is still being taught at The Bristol Old Vic Theatre School and if it's good enough for them, it's got to be good enough for you to at least give it a try.

This strange little technique will prevent you from any odd looking emotional leakage in the legs and it will give your voice a rich and sonorous tone helping you to communicate a great sense of gravitas and control. Unlike all the other exercises we have done where I asked to tense you legs arms or back only to find that your breathing is impaired, by 'squeezing your lemon' your breathing is actually improved. This is because you are tipping your pelvis forward as you do it straightening out, ever further, your breathing apparatus.

Of all these six points of posture this is my favourite largely because by doing this you become confident within an instant.

If you are ever in a situation where you need a quick burst of resolve, squeeze your lemon and you will go at it with an amazing sense of self-assurance. The trick with this one is to get into the habit of doing it and before you know it, any time you are faced with a challenging situation you will butt clench automatically and give yourself the boost you need to address whatever challenge you face and with full force.

In fact, my belief in this technique is so ardent that I will go as far as to say:

If you squeeze your butt cheeks together at the right time it will change the course of your life

An incredible claim you might think. But consider this; how many times a day do you have situation to deal with where you need a burst of courage, gumption or guts. Perhaps you have to say something to someone that is not easy to discuss. Perhaps you need to make a difficult phone call. You might need to confront somebody about something. Well, if you were to squeeze your lemon beforehand you will have a more commanding presence and a greater sense of self-assurance. With all these things in place you are in a much better emotional state to deal with that situation with a greater sense of courage and commitment.

When we stand in front of a problem and deal with it well, and indeed come out of it with the result we wanted, we create a mini win for ourselves. With each mini win your self-esteem is raised and with each mini win you are taking your life in a slightly different direction than if you hadn't dealt with the situation in hand.

Over the years think how the direction of your life will have changed for the positive.

In general it is a fantastic tool for dealing with the everyday difficulties life tends to throw at you. With direct relevance to your auditions it will give you a great boost of confidence right when you most need it. Just remember...

If in doubt squeeze your lemon!

And now, at last, what to do with your...

Hands!

Firstly...

Never stick your hands in your pockets.

Never stand with your hands on your hips.

Never fold your arms.

Never stand with your hands behind your back.

Never have your hands resting in front of your crotch.

And never, never, never stand with your hands by your sides!

Some of the above are better than others but dealing with each in turn let me tell you why all of the options listed will not help you.

Hands in pockets

In short you will look like you have something to hide by not having your hands on show. Also, by having your hands stuffed into your pockets you will be restricting your ability to gesticulate. Remember body language has incredible power as a device for communication – 55%! With your hands in your pockets you will look rigid, shifty and uncommunicative. As well as this your shoulders will hunch, your breathing will become restricted and our thought processes will be impaired as a result. So don't do it!

Hands on your hips

This is power-posturing which is much better done before you go in for your audition. By making yourself a bigger physical presence and raising your height as you do it in situ you will give the impression of someone wishing to take charge. Needless to say the fight or flight part of your interviewers brain will flash red. Directors are more likely to avoid a person who looks like they might threaten their authority.

Arms folded

Well, you tell me!

By folding your arms in front of you, you are putting up a huge barrier between you and the person auditioning you. It looks defensive and, as with hands in pockets, you are preventing yourself from using your arms to gesticulate. Also with the nerves of the situation you are likely to keep your arms folded. I call this locking and blocking because by locking your arms together, you are blocking effective communication.

Hands behind back

There is no doubt about it, this position will give you more confidence. For example, police are trained to stand like this so that they feel and project confidence but do you really want to look like a copper on the beat as you stand waiting to sing? Also, for reasons I am about to explain in the last section, with your arms in this position you will be impairing your ability to think and communicate effectively.

Hands resting in front of your crotch

This posture can make people look a little penitent, like a schoolgirl/boy standing in front of their headmaster while receiving a bollocking that they know they deserve.

I have seen this position used more by women than men but I would avoid it because it can sometimes look like you are infantilising yourself – making yourself come across as sweet and innocent may make you feel more secure in the moment, but I would suggest that by appealing to the parenting instincts of your interviewers you are giving away your power and losing status.

Hands by your side

By standing with your hands by your side you are going to trigger your fight or flight mechanism. Think about it, you're standing still with no barrier to protect your vital organs. You won't want to be a static target so your good old fight or flight will start making you shuffle around, maybe even pace about the floor so that you become a moving target. Also your energy will be falling from you and into the ground plus you will look a complete dork!

Along with all that, as with having your hands in your pockets, behind your back or covering your crotch you will be slowing your heart rate, breathing rate and electrical activity in the brain. Your facial expressions will become flattened as will your tone of voice. All in all you will be stripping yourself of all that aids you in communicating well.

So don't do it!

Why does all this happen just because you have your hands in these positions? The most simple explanation is that those arms that you have hanging down by your side, backside or privates are filled with blood and all that blood is doing is sloshing around your hands making the flow of said blood around the body more sluggish and impeding your circulation.

Having gone on at great length about what not to do with your hands I am now going to give you the most simple technique called 'BBC arms' that will put your hands in the optimum position as you stand in front of your audition panel.

Do this now:

Stand with happy feet

Pull your string

Lift your chest up, put your shoulders back

Squeeze your lemon

And now... lightly place one hand in the other and rest them against your stomach on or above your naval.

You now have BBC arms, so called because weather girls, reporters and TV presenters on the BBC will have their hands in this position as a default when they speak to camera. Don't believe me? Check it out next time you watch the news.

As you stand in this position you will have a fantastic sense of being really centred. And because your arms have been lifted you are aiding your blood to be circulated more efficiently, raising your pulse, breathing rate and mental acuity. With your hands crossed lightly over your belly you are placing a gentle barrier that will keep you fight or flight in check. What's more, you will be further winning the trust of the people interviewing you because you are sending out the clear body language message that you are trustworthy.

Are BBC arms really that powerful? I assure you that they are.

As your hands rest against you stomach you are drawing the attention of the interviewers fight or flight system to your viscera, in just the same way as when you use part two of the open handshake. And as you speak you will be gesticulating outward, opening yourself up. The message you are sending out is clear. All my defences are down, I feel safe and at ease in your company so I have no need for any protection from you. And just as I described earlier, their mirroring neuron will replicate your emotional state so they will be open and at ease with *you*.

Do this now:

Stand in front of a full-length mirror

Stand with happy feet

Pull your string

Lift your chest up, put your shoulders back

Squeeze your lemon

Use BBC arms

Can you see how this is a great default posture? You look relaxed ready for action, open, affable, friendly, approachable and trustworthy.

Now drop your arms by your side.

The difference in the image you are presenting has just taken a massive leap in the wrong direction hasn't it? Instead of coming across as energized and focused you now seem more than a bit limp. You have drooped within an instant. And what happened to your energy? Yes, it dropped right down into the floor.

Go back to using BBC arms.

I know you can feel the difference instantly. Putting your arms in this position makes you feel comfortable, protected yet open at the same time.

I love BBC arms most when I am waiting for a musical intro

to play through before I burst into song. The extra bonus of BBC arms when waiting to sing is that it aids your breathing so that when you begin singing you will have ample air.

If I ever have to stand during the interview part of the interview I will have my BBC arms gently in place and gesticulate out when giving my answers.

Start using BBC arms today. You will find that people will be far more open to you, what you have to say and any suggestions you might make. Again, it will benefit you tremendously if you get used to doing this before you go into an audition. Finally...

What to do with your mouth

Do this now:

Stand in front of a full-length mirror

Stand with happy feet

Pull your string

Lift your chest up, put your shoulders back

Squeeze your lemon

Use BBC arms

And smile!

It's the cherry on the top of the cake. It acts as the glue that sticks together and legitimises all the other five parts of your positive posture package. Without a smile the rest of the positions are good but nowhere near as good.

Do this now:

Use all the parts of your positive posture package including the smile.

Now drop your smile.

The effect is immediate and undeniable. It's just not the same if you are not smiling.

There it is – my perfect posture package. I swear by it. I use it in life and every audition I ever attend. It puts me in a positive place internally and projects warmth, openness and a quiet confidence. But here's the thing...

The positive posture package will only really work its magic if you use it without thinking about using it. I really want you to start putting this stuff in place from now on. If you use the positive posture package for the next 21 days it will have gone deep into your subconscious competent memory – the bit of your memory that you use when you drive a car – you can do it without consciously thinking about it. Well, that's how the positive posture package works best. Get it engrained into your body so that you will use it automatically whenever you are in an audition situation. The same goes for 'Ready, Steady, Go'. Make it a part of you so that without thinking you utilize proprioceptive psychology to your great and everlasting benefit.

In his book, 'Winning Body Language' actor and communications trainer Mark Bowden goes into great detail about this subject. I highly recommend it as further reading.

Chapter 12

How to handle a re-call

So, using everything you have learnt in this book so far I can make the safe assumption that your first round audition will be a positive experience. You may not get the job but an audition that went well is money in the bank. It is good for your soul, your self-esteem and your long-term prospects.

Remember: An audition that goes well never goes away

Quite often you will be cast on the back of your initial audition particularly with commercials and guest appearances in TV shows. In theatre, one audition is quite commonly enough for a director to know if you are the person they want but most of the time you can expect a re-call. If you are auditioning for a West End musical you need to get your head around the notion that a first round audition can be followed six or seven recalls!

Now something very interesting happens in our heads when we have a recall. We get nearer the money, which, in our heads we can start spending- holidays, new laptops, a Caribbean Cruise - and most importantly we get nearer to actually being able to do the job! Two months in rep theatre playing the part of your dreams, a year on tour in your favourite musical of all time, a few weeks on a telly shooting in South Africa! All dizzying stuff. But as the prize draws nearer so our fight or flight complex becomes all the more over active. As the stakes become higher so do our anxiety levels and as we know we never audition at our best when we are anxious. So what can we do to stop this heightened nervousness?

My first tip to combat this is to keep doing what you already *been* doing:

- Know your sh#t!
- Know your values and use them to strengthen your mindset
- Use Ready Steady Go before you enter the audition room
- Use perfect posture as you stand in front of the panel
- Use your open handshake to reaffirm your qualities of openness and trustworthiness
- Finally, sock it to them for all your worth!

Certainly the first suggestion on that list will take on a new meaning for re calls. If you are auditioning for a particular part they are likely to give you sides to learn. Get these firmly under your belt and in your subconscious competent memory. Make it one less thing to worry about. As my old actor mate Jeffry Harmer always said, 'learn your lines and enjoy the day'.

If you are auditioning for a role in a musical you can expect to be given particular songs to learn and stretches of dialogue that you will need to be fully in command of.

But I want to give you even more techniques that are fantastic for keeping you focused, positive and in the moment.

All the stuff in the previous chapters that I have just listed are your bedrock tools for being in a great place in the audition scenario. They are the golden rules. What follow are golden options.

Some will work for you better than others. Try them all and eventually you will use – and keep using – the techniques that bring you results and those results will keep on coming.

The Internal Dynamo

When you are waiting for your turn at a recall it is perfectly natural to feel more than a little overwhelmed by the situation you find yourself in. All the same negative voices will sound in your head, you may notice your posture moving from 'ready, steady, go' to 'Jesus, just get me out of here'! Go to the golden rules, put that indeterminate smile on your face and know that 'you are meant to be right here, right now'. Soon you will be feeling back on track. You can add to this sense of even greater energy by using a technique I call the internal dynamo.

It is a simple piece of visualisation, easily within your capabilities and it acts a fantastic mind trick you can use on yourself to lift you from the negative to the positive while giving you a massive surge of 'Can Do' energy.

I want you to imagine that sitting in your sternum is a silver wheel pointing forward.

Now imagine the wheel begins to spin in an upward/ outward motion rapidly picking up speed and energy.

As it spins faster and faster imagine that the wheel turns

from silver to gold and then begins to radiate a wonderful warming light.

As you go through this simple exercise you will quickly feel your energy leap up and a gratifying sense of optimism and resolve fill you from your chest right through to the top of your head.

As with all these tools the best advice I can give you is to get used to using them before you need them. Don't actually wait until you have a second round audition before you try this. Put it into practice in every day life. For me I use the internal dynamo before I have to get up and give a motivational speech. It gives me the boost I need to grab the situation by the short and curlies!

I tend also to use it when I am waiting for a business meeting where the rewards stand to be quite significant and long lasting. It is a simple and highly potent way for me to banish any pre meeting blues or anxiety based lethargy.

I'm really keen for you to start feeling the benefit of using your inner dynamo so that, if it works for you, you can put it into place when you will benefit from it the most. So...

I know this seems a weird suggestion but, you know when you are supposed to be going out for the night and you're not quite in the mood? Try the inner dynamo and see how quickly it lifts your spirits.

You might be at work in your day job and having a burst of downheartedness. Try it when you have a lull in your spirits and note the difference it has on the way you feel.

I'm going to hand over to NLP practitioner Beth Parmar who taught me how to create confidence in two very distinct ways - one 'in the moment' and the other when prepping for the rigours of a recall.

Over to you Beth...

The game of confidence is won or lost in the mind. Our unconscious mind has a massive role in influencing how we feel, how we think and whether or not we believe we are going to be any good at the task in hand. NLP (Neuro Linguistic Programming) is all about understanding how we can harness the power of the unconscious mind by learning some simple tips and strategies to make sure that we are always able to be at our best even in tricky or nerve-racking situations.

Many NLP techniques focus on the power of visualisation. This is because our unconscious mind actually believes whatever it is that we visualise and it makes up around 95% of our brain. So that little conscious voice in our head telling us that what we are visualising isn't actually real can get drowned out pretty quick once we get competent at visualising to our advantage.

Anchoring

The first technique I want to share with you is called

'anchoring'. Anchoring is all about linking a specific action with a positive feeling. It has its roots way back with Russian scientist Dr Pavlov who carried out some behavioural experiments with a group of dogs. You've probably heard the story of how he gathered his group of dogs together at mealtimes and rang a bell at the exact same time that he put their food in front of them.

He continued to do this at each mealtime for around two weeks. Everyday the same – he rang the bell and put their food down for them to eat. At the end of the two-week period he changed the experiment slightly and he just rang the bell and didn't put the food down. What happened physiologically for the dogs was that they still produced saliva and were totally physically ready to eat the food even though there was no sign of it. The ringing of the bell had been enough of a prompt for their unconscious brains to start telling the body to get ready to eat their food. The bell had become an anchor for the dogs, an anchor that linked hearing a bell ringing to eating food.

In our daily lives we have lots of these anchors that have been set up out of habit over time to create physiological responses on our bodies. How about when you hear a certain song on the radio and without thinking tears form in your eyes, or a huge grin appears on your face? What about smells like freshly cut grass, or your Nan's famous apple pie that can create feelings of nostalgia about your childhood perhaps?

When you look at certain photos of your family, friends or of holidays you have been on, do you get the stirrings of love, pride or happiness? All of these are examples of how we anchor sounds, smells or pictures to feelings in our bodies without any conscious effort. The feelings come because that is how we have unconsciously trained our bodies to react.

So what has this got to do with preparing for an audition then? Well, if we know that it is possible to unconsciously create a link between seeing, hearing or smelling something and experiencing a particular feeling, wouldn't it be useful if we could consciously create positive anchors for ourselves to use in situations where we could do with a little more calmness, confidence, or focus? This is where an NLP concept called kinaesthetic anchoring comes in very handy.

What this is all about is training our brain to make a connection between us doing something physical, like squeezing a knuckle for example, and feeling a particular positive sensation in our bodies. It's a very simple exercise to do and one that I think everyone should have up their sleeve for tricky situations. There are two things you need to decide upon before doing this exercise. Firstly you need to decide which part of your body you are going to touch. I suggest something like a knuckle (on your left hand if you are right handed or on you right hand if you are left handed). You can squeeze your knuckle with your other hand. I like to press with two fingers on the top and the thumb below. Equally you could squeeze the fleshy part between your thumb and index finger, *or maybe even your earlobe. It needs to be something you do easily and subtly, as you will more than likely have to use it when other people are around.*

Secondly I need you to think of a time when you felt the feeling that you wish to anchor. For the purposes of getting into the right state for an audition, it is probably most useful for you to set up a calmness anchor. I think everyone should have a calmness anchor they can use in tricky situations to help them calm down and think more clearly. So think of a time in the past where you felt really calm. It could be a particular view, perhaps a great holiday, any time where you were relaxed, calm and carefree. I have to say at this point don't confuse calmness with sleepiness. They are two different things and we don't want to be making you feel sleepy when you press your anchor when you should just be calming down.

So now you have decided on these two important things, sit comfortably, free of distractions, close your eyes and get ready to press your anchor point. Don't press it yet. Now think of that time when you felt calm. Go back in time and relive that experience as if it was happening right now. Notice what you can see, feel and hear as you feel calm, notice where you feel calm in your body as you relive the experience. Once you are feeling calm then press your anchor and continue to keep it pressed all the time you are feeling calm. Notice as much detail as you can about that calm experience. What are you seeing, what is going on around you, how does the calmness feel in your body? Keep reliving the experience and keep pressing your anchor. Keep it pressed until you feel that the calmness is subsiding a little and then release your anchor and open your eyes.

OK that was the first part of the exercise. How did you find it? Easy? Straightforward? Did you get the feelings of calmness? You'll need to repeat exactly what you have just done a few more times – six more to be precise. If you are happy with your experience you have chosen then continue to use that. If you would prefer to use a different calm experience then feel free to change it. So long as it is still something calm. You could always alternate between two or more calm experiences – the choice is yours.

This exercise works on repetition. The more you establish the anchor, the stronger it gets and the more useful it becomes as a resource to calm down. Also incidentally, the more you use your anchor, the stronger it will become as each time you use it and calm down it strengthens the association between pressing your anchor and feeling calm. If you don't use it though, it obviously won't get any stronger and the connection may be lost over time. So the message is clear on this one – use it or lose it!

Get ready to try it again. Close your eyes and go back to that time that you felt really calm. Relive the experience in detail until you feel calmness in your body, then press your anchor and keep it held. This time I want you to imagine you can turn all the feelings up, like you're turning dials on a mixing deck. Turn those feelings of calmness right up, letting them spread inside your body, making you feel really calm, and really relaxed. Enjoy those feelings of calmness as you relive that experience of total calmness, seeing what you saw, and hearing what you heard. Keep reliving the experience and keep pressing your anchor. Keep it pressed until you feel that the calmness is subsiding a little and then release your anchor and open your eyes.

You now need to complete the remaining repetitions to establish the anchor and make it strong. Really take the time to do the exercise fully. Don't skip it and come back to it if you can help it. Take just a few moments to take part in this process and establish yourself a really useful resource anchor so you can use it at anytime you need an instant hit of calmness. Very useful when preparing for scary and nerve racking situations.

Ok how did that feel? Do you feel calmer right now? Easy wasn't it? It's a good idea to keep repeating this process whenever you have a few quiet minutes to yourself. Now we need to test your anchor. What I want you to do now is to try just pressing your anchor and then just notice what is happening in your body. Are you starting to feel the physical sensations of calmness? Maybe your stomach feels more relaxed, maybe your shoulders relax and drop a bit, maybe you just feel clearer in your head. Any of these signs (or maybe you've got other physical signs) is good and each time you use *your anchor or do more repetitions of the setting up of it, it will get stronger and stronger. That's the beauty of this exercise.*

You can create and set up as many anchors as you like. As well as a calmness one, you could set up a confidence one, drawing on the experience of a time when you felt really confident about something. You could also try one for improving your get up and go if you are struggling to motivate yourself to get going. Just think of a time when you did feel motivated to get out and about getting things done, maybe when you were doing something physical like going for a run or going to the gym and were feeling really alive and active. Remember to use a different knuckle or part of your body for different feelings you are trying to anchor – you don't want to get them mixed up!

The Circle of Excellence

Another technique I want to share with you is called The Circle of Excellence. This is a visual tool that works on influencing the unconscious mind to boost confidence in a nerve-racking situation. It's particularly useful for when you are getting ready to stand up and perform in front of other people. Perfect for an audition scenario.

The first step in this exercise is for you to visualise a circle like a spot light beam on the stage where you are about to stand and deliver your performance. This technique works particularly well if you can visualise this circle in the actual room you will be performing in. Perhaps you've been in the room before, or you can get the chance to take a look before you're ready to go in. As you focus on this circle in front of you, visualise what the circle would look like if it were filled with colours, shapes, textures or objects you associate with confidence. Perhaps you see it full of sparkling light, maybe gold or silver, perhaps bright coloured shapes, your favourite animal, it's entirely up to you − it's your visualisation. Just think what your circle of excellence would be filled with?

Focus on how your circle would look and then when you are ready, step into that circle and allow all of the colours, shapes and textures to be absorbed into your body, filling it with all that positive confident energy. Really visualise what your body would look like it if was full of the shapes and colours you imagined.

For me personally, confidence is a gold liquid. When I need to get up in front of groups of people and speak, I visualise my circle being full of glowing gold liquid and then as I visualise it filling my body from my toes to the top of my head. This makes me feel so strong and confident that my nerves quickly dissipate and I am able to give a more credible performance. Play around with the images until you come up with one that gives you the strongest feelings of confidence. Practice it prior to your interview so you can get used to stepping into the circle and visualising the feelings filling your body. You may find that you have different colours and textures for different situations in the same way as you can have different anchors. That's fine – just remember which one is which so you don't get them confused!

Thank you Beth.

Trust me when I say, this stuff is magic. I highly recommend that you try Beth's techniques out for yourself.

More than that, if you want to give yourself a great start at all your auditions right from the beginning of your career use all the techniques that have been listed in the book so far.

They work and if you use them, *you* will work.

Part 4

The business of 'show business'

In this final section we look at all the different types of audition you will be attending and breaking down the various demands each strand of the business will make on you. We will be looking at auditioning for musical theatre, screen, self tape and commercial castings.

But first we need to take a look at that all important much-maligned sector of showbiz that acts as a conduit between you and the all important auditions you need to get to enable you to work.

Chapter 13

Agents!

So I want you to cast your mind back to those two people I befriended at my Guildhall audition back in 1983, Bill and Rachel.

You'll remember Rachel went on to enjoy and, indeed continues to enjoy a full and varied career in the business. And Bill? Well, I'm going to tell you what happened to Bill right now.

Bottom line – he eventually became a student at Webber Douglas, spent seven happy years as an actor and then took a left hand turn within the industry and became an agent. And about eleven years ago, he became MY agent!

After our two years as pen pals we eventually lost contact with each other. About twenty years later, I was casting around for a new agent and had written a letter to The Talent Group. On making my follow up phone call was greeted by none other than Bill Petrie. And the rest as they say is history.

Along with Joe Hutton and all the team at the BWH agency I have been with Bill from that time to this.

When I mentioned to Bill that I was writing this book he was very keen to be a part of the project. From my own point of view it is a fantastic opportunity to give new actors a greater insight into how an agent operates and the many things that need to be taken into consideration when choosing your agent and working with them for the duration of your professional association.

The BWH agency has become hugely successful and Bill was going to find it difficult to find the time to sit and write a full chapter from start to finish so I decided to take him for a drink armed with a stack of questions and a recording device. We had a fascinating discussion, which I have transcribed but I warn you, while my questions are broad in their scope the answers Bill gives are detailed, thought-provoking and challenging. This sound advice from a highly respected industry professional at times may prick your conscience. It certainly gave *me* food for thought.

I hope you enjoy our discussion...

What advice would you give to an actor choosing an agent?

The most important thing to remember is that you are choosing to employ them. You wouldn't employ someone you knew nothing about would you? So in seeking an agent the first thing to do is arm yourself with as much information about them as possible.

Do your research on the agency, the clients that they have on their books and the kind of work that those clients are doing. If that is the type of work that you want to do then there is a good chance that agent can get you the sort of work you would be happy with.

You can see by going through Spotlight if an agent has a lot of clients working in America, for example, or for the RSC. If an agent has loads of people performing in musical theatre and that's the area you want to work in then you should seek them out for a meeting. The sort of agent who can get you work in physical theatre might not be the same agent who can get you into The Manchester Royal Exchange so knowing what you want to do and seeking out the agent who can set up the right kind of meeting for you is essential in choosing the right agent for you.

So you have managed to secure a meeting. What next?

Well, then it's about do you get on with them. Aside from what work they might be able to get you, the agent/client relationship is an extremely personal one so it is vital that you feel comfortable in their company. The sort of questions you need to ask yourself are:

Do you like them?

Do you think they like you?

Do you feel that they listened to you during your meeting?

Do you get the feeling that they will try and facilitate your ambitions?

If the answers to those questions are yes, then you have every reason to sign with them and give it a go.

Other questions you need to consider:

Do you find them frightening?

Would you foresee a relationship where they made themselves unapproachable?

Do you feel you could call them with a problem?

If the answer to those questions is no... keep looking!

Another major decision is do you want to go with an agent with years of experience behind them or go for a new young gun who is bursting with energy and enthusiasm? I know that you learn something new everyday as an agent. For example I know that, being in my 50s, I am a far better agent than I was in my thirties just through the experiences I have gained from actually doing the job.

Should you go with an agent who hasn't seen you perform?

I think the same principles should apply. Do your research and see how you feel when you meet them.

But the received wisdom was that if you go with someone who hasn't seen you act is a waste of time.

Well, an agent might go on a hunch. Of course it helps if they can see you because they'll be equipped with a much broader idea of what you can do, but if you're coming out of a decent drama school after three years, an agent would assume that the actor would be reasonably well equipped with a broad foundation of skills.

You'd assume they could speak in RP and it would be fair to assume that they have a fair modicum of talent. And then if you meet that actor and you like them, if you click then you can work from the point of view that casting directors will like them to and you would be happy to sell them with that as a starting point.

I stress though, for this to be worthwhile the agent has to be a decent one. If they are well connected with a good reputation they will be able to get you seen, and if they have agreed to take you on not withstanding whether they have seen you or not they will put you up for things in the hope that you will get seen and that you get booked.

The problem for both agents and performers is that there are simply too many young actors coming out of drama school every year and not enough agents that work at a sufficiently high level in the business to supply them with the sort of work they might be looking for.

What can an actor do to help their agent in getting auditions?

They should be going out to see theatre as often as they can afford – and that shouldn't just be going to see their friends from drama school in some fringe venue at the end of the Piccadilly Line. They need to know what's going on at the National, what's going on at the RSC, who the directors are in all these places, who the new writers are at the Royal Exchange and the Donmar.

They should go and see the important productions that people are talking about and have opinion about them. Then they should to write to the casting director of that production. Nothing too complicated, 'I recently saw the show you cast, I really enjoyed it, it was a great performance etc', and then ask if they would keep your CV and photo on record and keep you in mind for any future castings.

They have to read plays, classics and modern. They have to keep fit. They have to keep mixing with actors – not just hang with their work colleagues from their secondary job at the call centre, restaurant or bar.

It is essential that they keep their ear to the ground about what is happening in the business and what opportunities might be out there that they want to tell their agent about.

And they have to write letters/emails. My old drama teacher said you have to write two letters every day.

They have to know who the up and coming writers are and who the up and coming directors are. Staying on top of who the current movers and shakers in the business are a must. By writing letters or emails to them you will be getting your name out there and slowly building awareness.

There will come a time when you have a sufficiently high profile when you should stop writing off to people, but if you are just starting out then you should be sending out stuff diligently and daily.

In short, you have to arm yourself with as much knowledge as possible about who's who, who's where and what they are doing and when, while creating your own network of contacts by writing off. It's not rocket science but a great deal of young actors seem unwilling to do it. If you are prepared to put in the hard work in this way you will be putting yourself way ahead of your competitors.

Does an actor having a second job cause a problem for their agent?

Yes and no. When an actor is solvent and not worrying about the state of their finances that certainly takes away the panic and desperation that can creep in if they haven't been busy for a while. But yes, there can be a significant downside. I understand that most actors will have to bring in extra money by taking a secondary job but the real trick here is in striking the right balance.

Ultimately, you have to remember that first and foremost you are an actor.

You are not a waiter, you are not someone who works in a call centre, you're not a barman or an office temp. You are an actor servicing your career by taking a job – that is it.

Never get too comfortable in your second job. Never let yourself be defined by your second job and never, ever, ever, ever let your second job interfere with your first. The minute your second job starts to take priority over your career as an actor you are basically finished. It usually takes about five years for the transition to occur before you finally give up the business but in the meantime you will struggle with trying to be a servant of two masters.

If you are always calling your agent with lots of days when you're not available or you're going on holiday, if there is a high pressure situation and a casting director is on the phone to me saying, 'We've a casting tomorrow and I've had people drop out, I've got two spaces and I need two people to fill them who have you got for me? The last person who is going to spring to mind is someone who's availability can't be guaranteed because they have so many shifts in a call centre that you have to always work around.

The name of the actor that spring to mind is the actor who every time you say, 'You've got a meeting at 9.30 tomorrow. You need to be at such and such a place, you need to read this, and you need to do your research between now and then and they say, 'Fine', that's the actor you will always go to'. They then put the phone down and do all the necessary work. They do their research, they find out about the director, the theatre company, writer, any historical references they need to know, they read the play, learn their lines, they find out where they're going, they dress appropriately and show their personality.

That is the kind of actor you constantly push because they never let you down. And an actor like that will never ask themselves when they should call their agent because their agent is always calling them.

If you move from being fully focussed as an actor to losing your drive and shifting your priorities, pretty soon both jobs will suffer. You won't be able to do either of them right. (Paul's comments in the previous chapters about this are sound and right. Do something you love by all means but it must have flexibility- preferably be your own boss and you will always be in control of where you want to be and when).

Agents need their actors to say 'I'll be there'. Be one of those actors and you will get suggested far more regularly and get more auditions as a result.

Many actors feel they don't get the sort of auditions they were expecting from their agent. Why does this happen?

Ok, so I'll take you right back to where we started. Did they do the right sort of research on their agent before they joined them. If they are not getting the sort of auditions they were hoping for I would suggest that they did not carry out due diligence in that respect.

Also it helps to take a realistic view of your status within the business and work accordingly.

I always say that an actor should know his status within the business at any given time. That status can and will change, going both up and down. If you know what you are right for and what opportunities you can reasonably expect your agent to get for you then you will be happy. Understand that at the moment you may not get a leading role or the next supporting role down because in a movie producers can't get finance on you because you might not have the reputation you need to secure those type of high profile roles.

Nowadays your status as an actor is linked to many things. Dreadful as it is to contemplate, you may not have enough followers on Twitter or Facebook for example (More and more we get asked about numbers of followers on social media platforms).

If an actor has a realistic understanding of their status within the business they will stop beating their head against a brick wall hoping to be put up for stuff which, currently, they don't have the clout for.

If you are not a leading man in the West End yet, you're not going to get in for the leading roles. With time, as you get more work and you gain more experience and exposure, then expect the big stuff but in the meanwhile, bide your time and think of the bigger picture.

If you are going to commit your whole adult working life

as an actor it is of great benefit to understand that it is not a sprint, it's a marathon. Obviously, there are no guarantees but knowing where you are placed within the business and having the patience to allow your career to grow will eventually bear fruit and save you a great deal of frustration along the way.

If you have realistic expectations you will always be happy with the auditions your agent gets for you.

Do you think a lot of actors have unrealistic expectations then?

I would say yes and add that actors who live with other actors can often have their view somewhat skewed by the people they share a flat with!

If for example, your flat mate is a six foot, willowy blonde model type actress and you are a five foot six, rotund and brunette, every time your flatmate gets an audition don't think that they should be seeing you for the part as well. Don't phone your agent and say, 'Cheek by Jowl are doing a production of The Merchant Of Venice and my flatmate is up for Portia, can I get seen for it too?' The answer will invariably be no because you are not right for the part.

Know who you are, what you are and what you would be good casting for.

I had a client call me up once and she said, 'Can you try and get me seen for this show' and I said, 'We'll do our best what is it' and she said 'Five Guys Named Mo'. And I'd seen

'Five guys Named Mo' many times and I said, 'well what part?' and she said, 'Well, I don't know but I've just heard it's very good and they're doing it at Stratford East,' and so I said, 'Well, I think that might be a bit of a problem,' and she says, 'Why, why?' and so I said, 'Well, I think the clue's in the title'. And she got all funny with me, 'What do you mean, what do you mean?' she said.

I didn't want to hurt her feelings or make her feel silly so I took my time with her.

'Well,' I said, 'there's only five people in the show',

'So!'

"And they're all called Mo',

'And?'

And they're all guys'.

'Oh', she said.

It makes for a lovely little anecdote but in reality it's quite hard to keep respect for any actor in that type of situation.

Don't panic just because you've heard that there is an audition and phone your agent pleading to, 'get me seen, get me seen, get me seen'.

In fairness, a knee jerk response to a friend getting an audition is not always a bad thing – but it is always a bad thing most of the time!

Generally it's because you hear that there is an audition for something and you ask your agent to get you seen for the project without doing proper research. (there's that word again).

No agent will mind if you've heard something on the grapevine and you call them with an informed request but most of the time I guarantee that if you look into things properly you'll end up not making the call to your agent in the first place.

This is a great way of avoiding unnecessary frustration and heartache and putting your relationship with your agent under strain. A poorly researched request to be seen for an inappropriate audition will just waste your agent's time and you'll go down in their estimation.

How often should you call your agent?

There is no set rule or measure for this. I think it should be organic. It will find its own place depending on how busy you are and how castable you are. Again, does the agent like you, have you done well in previous auditions, if that's the case, you will get more phone calls coming your way instead of the other way round.

But I would say, if you haven't heard from your agent for a time it is worth while to call. If the agency has too many clients or the number of clients has grown significantly since you joined them, or a block of their actors are doing very well and are keeping them busy you can go out of their mind and you can get forgotten about. In those situations it is a good idea to give them a nice friendly gentle nudge...now and again. And maybe now and again is once a month? Maybe it's once every two weeks or so, it just depends on your relationship. But I genuinely think if you don't have that as a concern you have picked well with your agent and they have picked well in their client.

What about when actors feel they are not getting enough auditions?

There are many people involved with the decision to call you in for an audition for something. It's not just the agent deciding whether or not they want to put you up for a particular project or not.

But firstly, what I would say is, if your agent does get you an audition, for God's sake go to the audition!

If you say, 'I don't want to do that,' or 'I can't make that because I've got a role play that day,' you are missing out on countless other auditions that might come your way because you didn't walk through the door.

Every time you go for an audition, you're auditioning for another ten, twenty other jobs. The director goes off and does ten jobs that you don't know about, you might have done a good audition but you didn't get that part but they'll remember you. The casting director goes off and does ten jobs, there might be a writer goes off and does ten jobs. Go to the audition. You don't have to accept every job that comes your way by any means but get seen and, hopefully, you'll be remembered for other things.

With regard to younger actors, if you don't fit what they're casting at the moment, you are going to get less auditions. No agent will waste their time and their clients' time by putting them up for stuff they just won't get. If you've had ten auditions and you haven't booked a job, you're going to get less auditions. If you get three bookings out of the first ten auditions you get, you're going to work, people will see you, you'll have stuff on your CV that you can talk about. For those reasons, you're going to jump up a rung on the ladder.

Now, when a casting director who's employed by a producer and chosen by the director has two days for auditions for a play they have to choose very wisely. Because if she brings in a whole load of actors and the producers and director see that they haven't worked for a year, they will turn to their casting director and say, 'Why are you bringing me actors who have not worked? They don't work. I don't want these actors. Get me actors who have just worked at the Donmar, I want the people who have finished at the National. That's who I want and that's what I'm paying you as a casting director to do.'

So in many ways it doesn't matter how well an agent might get on with a casting director. I could suggest an actor for a play till I'm blue in the face. They will eventually make their decision not just based on the talent of the actor but on what the director and producer want.

A casting director has to make sure that they get more work too so they must respect the wishes of their creative team or else they won't be trusted with another project from them. It really is quite a complex line of decisions that are taken before you get the go ahead to send your client along to audition. Like I said, it's not just about the client, it's not just about the agent.

So why else do actors start getting less auditions?

A major reason why an actor will be seen less and less is because they prove themselves to be poor timekeepers or have developed a sloppy attitude toward punctuality.

If you are continually late, that casting director won't see you again and that will hit the number of auditions you get seen for straight away. One casting director will cast 20 or 30 projects through the course of their career, but if you proved yourself unreliable you will never be considered for anything again because casting directors will always remember when somebody lets them down.

In fact late arrivals and no shows are becoming so prevalent nowadays that one top-casting director stipulates in her emails 'Your client must audition at the appointed time. Times will not be rearranged for the convenience of the actor and no shows are unacceptable'.

Staggering as it might be to understand, nowadays people just don't turn up.

They will cite illness, childcare issues or can't change a shift at work, all of which is understandable. However, if you are a Dutch production company and you decide to cast from the UK you spend money on a casting director, who books a studio *for two days, that is already a large spend.*

If the casting director has to go back to them to say five people didn't show up it looks bad for both her and the agents whose clients failed to get there. The casting director will then think twice about going to that agent again and you will, likely as not, never get seen by the casting director for other projects. And then the actor will sit and wonder why they aren't getting enough auditions when actually the responsibility will lie with them.

It's a phrase heard often when actors get together, 'My agent's useless'. What is your view on this?
There might well be some agents who are useless. But think about this: It might be you that is useless!

On the last call or audition you went for you might not have been off book, lots of actors go into an audition and just wing it. Let's say you have a casting come through where you are given three pages of dialogue to learn. They may go in kind of knowing their lines, they will have spent a bit of time on it and when they can just about remember the dialogue think that they are prepared. Make no mistake, just being able to remember the lines does not make you audition ready.

When you go into the interview and they can see you struggling to remember your lines, they'll switch off – and that all goes back to focus and commitment.

You're not just trying to learn lines, you have to think about the character that you are trying to create. You should be striving to make it unique, exciting and something that is different from what the director has envisaged so that when you give your audition you engage the directors imagination and inspire him to give you the job. That level of commitment to an audition takes a great deal of time. Finishing a bar shift at 11.30pm getting up the next day at 8am, sitting in front of your lines for an hour and getting to your audition is not enough.

As an agent I make a point of showing due respect to my casting directors and the producers they are working for by only taking on clients who fully prepare and who arrive promptly for their appointed slot. It is a waste of our time to try and get someone through the door when the casting director knows that they were a no-show on the previous set of auditions that they had arranged.

More broadly, if an actor really feels they are not getting enough auditions the actor should look at themselves and start to analyse why that is the case – having the courage to put themselves in the middle of the equation.

The default will be to blame their agent. But no agent can stay in business if they not getting a significant amount of work for the clients on their books. If you are not getting auditions take a long look in the mirror and ask yourself these questions:

Am I really doing everything I can to be a good and reliable client?

Am I fully informed about what is going on in the business?

Am I writing to people often enough?

Am I always available for auditions at the drop of a hat?

Am I properly prepared, off book and ready to go.

Do I spend more time in the pub than you do in the gym or going to the theatre?

These are all relevant questions the actor should ask themselves. If you are asking yourself these questions right now and are starting to feel uncomfortable with the answers then you know you have to do something to address those issues.

Is lateness for auditions really becoming so commonplace?

Sadly yes and not just lateness, absenteeism!

I had a situation with a lovely casting director, old school, brilliant and very selective. She really knows what she is doing and will only see two people for each role that she is casting. On this occasion she was casting a commercial for Belgium and out of the two clients I sent up for it, neither of them showed up. A 100% no show from the clients at BWH!

Now I have a long history with this particular casting director and we are very fond of each other and, while she still uses me, that situation put a huge strain on our professional relationship.

As for the two no-show clients?

I had a conversation with one of them and gently pointed out that I got the feeling he wasn't really committed anymore and that this might be a good time to get out of the game. He was 30, running his own business, he had a serious girlfriend and it turned out that he agreed, it was a good time to bow out. He was a good example of somebody who thinks they want to be an actor and hopes to just pick and chose his auditions. Sadly, a solid career never happens for someone like him because he was never working enough and, sorry to have to say it, that was due to his overall lack of focus.

The other guy, it turned out, was working as a night manager in a hotel and the night before the audition there was actually a fire where he worked. The long and the short of it was he was up all night dealing with that and when he got home he collapsed into bed and couldn't wake up. Any actor worth his salt in that situation will get themselves to their appointment even if they have to turn up covered in burning coals with their hair alight. He was let go.

Why do you think so many people who leave drama school leave the business within five years?

The first thing people do when they leave drama school is to, maybe, get a normal job to pay the bills, fair enough. But I'll say it again, it's all about striking the right balance. Don't get caught in a call centre and just hanging around with your work mates who know nothing about theatre, they will not stimulate you. If you are not very careful you can get wrapped up into what we call 'the normal world' where you are surrounded by normal people and you get used to doing normal things. But I don't think actors are normal, whether they like it or not, they have something in them which sets them apart from the majority of society. And an actor should not be mixing with the normal people they should be observing them. I appreciate that at the same time you've got to have a life but an actor should never accept a 'normal' life.

Actors are special, actors are separate. When you decide to become an actor you really chose a vocation and while there is a great deal of isolation and heartache in an actors life I can't help feeling that is a vital price to pay if you want to do well.

The strange thing about the normal world is that it has an incredible hold on people. If you make the decision to break free from it, it will do all it can to pull you back into the fold.

You asked about why so many finish drama school and then fall away from the business. Well, let's say a person will get a place in the drama school of their choice. They will leave home, moving away from all that has been familiar to them and the influences that have shaped them thus far.

During the course of their training and as a direct result of it they will change. Their accent will become more RP, they will stand a bit taller because they're doing their Alexander technique. They will move differently because they develop a great sense of their own physicality, their frame of reference becomes broader, their intellect will become used to being challenged and stretched, their sense of self esteem will, rightly, become greatly enhanced, their ability as a performer will be hugely enriched and eventually, they come out at the other end of a three year course and they have become an actor.

A large number of these people will then go straight back home and in a very short period of time they return to what they were before they went to drama school in the first place.

They fall back into their natural speech rhythm, lose the physical awareness they spent so long developing. They slip back into whatever role and positioning they had with their family and their friends and are surrounded by and become everything they wanted to grow away from. They lose touch with their ambition and can soon fall into a state of drift.

The greatest tragedy of this is that they lose touch with the person they allowed themselves to become, the very person who would have helped them live that dream, the true actor within them and this is very troublesome.

The best example of this I can give; we saw this young actor in his final showcase, he had a great voice, looked fantastic and had a considerable raw ability. We were very impressed so we took him on. What we didn't really take on board was that he came from the West Country. The minute he left his drama school he went back home to Newton Poppleford and the next time we saw him he was speaking like one of the Wurzles and walking about like a fish wife!

The problem was that every time he came up to London for an audition he brought his West Country accent with him and people had a difficult time of thinking of him as anything other than a country bumpkin because he didn't move and sound neutral enough. Any of the skills he had learnt to walk the neutral line had been expunged; all his training had effectively disappeared.

When you come out of your training you need to move forward with it bringing all you learnt with you. Going back to where you came from will turn you back into what you were, except you will suffer the unhappiness of losing touch with all that you had allowed yourself to become.

So why do so many drama students just go straight back home after their training?

The difficulty with that is that living in London is very, very expensive but the competition is so very fierce these days that you won't stand a chance as a young actor if you go back to your family home because you are taking yourself out of the fray.

I think the saddest thing to see is someone who thinks that they want to be an actor in their head but not in their heart. Really, they want other things more. The safety and the familiarity of home, they want the normal things, to be with their friends, have relationships, they want the security of a steady income. All the things a person is entitled to in life but all the things that must come second if you are going to chose the life of an actor. You've got to have laser like focus, and 100% commitment – a part of that commitment is to understand the sacrifices you will need to make at the beginning of your career and continue to make throughout your whole life as an actor.

We have spoken a great deal about the difficulties associated with the hardships of being an actor. What are the challenges an actor has to face up to if they become successful?

If you are lucky to have success very quickly when you are young and fresh out of your drama school it can really screw with your head. Playing the lead in a high profile TV show or a feature film is the closest thing any one can experience to being royalty.

Let's say, you will be shooting for four months. Every morning there will be a chauffeur driven limousine waiting to take you to your location. You'll sit on the leather upholstered back seat, perhaps going over your lines when you get a phone call from one of the runners asking what you would like for your breakfast when you get to the location.

It gets better. As you arrive on the lot, if it's raining, there will be somebody running to open your car door with an umbrella so as you step out of the limo there is no chance of you getting wet. You get into your heated trailer and your coffee is waiting for you, just as you like it. There will be wardrobe people helping you off with your day clothes and helping you into your costume, all the while asking you polite questions and finding everything you say hugely interesting or fantastically amusing. You only need to ask for anything you want and it is brought to you... And you start to get used to it.

When you shoot your scene everybody will tell you how good, truthful, honest, or hilarious you were. In the bar that night a whole host of people from the production will be telling you just how great you are and how lucky the whole production is to have you...

And you start to believe it.

This stuff happens day in, day out for months on end and if you're not careful the whole situation creates a monster out of the humble grateful actor who shyly turned up for work on the first day four months previously! They can become demanding, ungrateful and basically spoilt. Danger signs are when the actor starts to say things like, 'My character wouldn't say that', 'My character wouldn't wear that', 'I don't want to come in at seven o'clock'.

The transformation rarely occurs on the first job but as success grows so does the actor's status and, in short, it can go to their head. This is something to be very wary of. When success comes it can be a wonderful experience but it can be short lived and if, during your time at the top, you have become difficult the come down can be terribly humiliating if you have been unpleasant or arrogant.

It will also affect your relationship with your agent if you start being difficult within the industry. Producers will be quick to call an actor's agent if they become arrogant or unpleasant or problematic sometimes leading to a difficult confrontation.

It's a terrible thing to take a client fresh from drama school, help them to achieve wonderful things only to see them blow it all by becoming a diva. In the past we have had to sit actors down and tell them their behaviour is not acceptable, that they've changed, that they have become demanding. Sometimes we actually let people go if they don't sort themselves out and change their attitude.

Another important thing to note if you are successful is that your success is achieved by combination of you and your team. Other agents will not be interested in you if you are unsuccessful, they will not seek out an actor who is not doing well. Only, when success strikes will other agents crawl out of the woodwork and show a desire to take you on and help you 'move forward'. But be careful.

Remember there is a reason why you're successful and it's not just you, it's the people and personalities that are around you working for you professionally. So don't break it up. Over my 25 years working as an agent I have seen many young actors on the rise, the hot new thing and looking back now, they just aren't there anymore. Their careers stalled and they disappeared. Occasionally I'll be at an industry bash and I'll be chatting with some of the old school agents and we might say 'Well, whatever happened to so and so? Where are they now?' And the answers that invariably come out fall into two categories. They became too difficult to work with and the success went to their head and they got involved in drink and drugs, or they left the agent who got them their initial success in the first place.

Have you got one last piece of advice?

At the risk of sounding a little sententious, I'm going to paraphrase Rudyard Kipling.

'If you meet with Triumph or Disaster learn to treat those two imposters just the same'.

An actor's life will be full of highs and lows and it doesn't matter who you are – international star or jobbing actor you will know good times and bad and the greatest likelihood is that your fortunes will continually change. I think it is those changes in fortune that make being an actor so exciting, so challenging but ultimately so rewarding. A good agent will guide you through the good times and support you through the tough times. So chose wisely and chose well. Good luck!

Chapter 14

Auditioning for musical theatre

For this chapter I have enlisted the help of one of our favourite and enduring West End musical performers Linzi Hateley.

We met during my time in Mamma Mia when I gave my Harry opposite her brilliant Donna. Her credit list is as vast as it is enviable.

She began her career playing the title role in the RSC's production of Carrie and went on to appear as Eponine in 'Les Miserables', the Narrator in Joseph and His Amazing Technicolor Dreamcoat, Rizzo in Grease, Roxy in Chicago and has most recently appeared as Helen in both the film and National Theatre production of London Road and played Charity in the number one tour of Barnum. So basically, she knows her stuff. We hooked up for a coffee and I plied her with the questions I thought any aspiring musical performer would ask if they had the chance to pick her brains. I'm sure you will find much to learn from her experience and expertise.

Linzi, what advice can you give to people starting out in the business hoping to break into the world of musical theatre?

That is an almost impossible question to answer. The business now is very different from the one I started out in and the business around the business has taken quite a toll on the jobbing performer who wants to work their way through the ranks. The minute you have any type of celebrity born (usually) of a TV presence you can get cast in a leading role in a musical so the parts most people are hoping to achieve go to someone with a famous face.

This is truer of the touring circuit but it still holds in the West End. This inconsistency breeds terrible frustration and disappointment for a lot of performers so a good starting point is to find things in your life that keep you motivated while what you really want to do isn't happening.

Whatever experiences you have will create a different dynamic within you as a person so live your life to the full and observe the changes that happen to you as a result. This will make you a person of depth with a rich pool of experience to draw from.

At the risk of sounding patronising I want to begin with a warning. I have been through what I am about to describe and I only mention it because I feel it is a vital lesson to learn.

When you're young and new to the game you feel you are invincible. And when you get that first West End job it is easy to fall under the impression that that is it, that you have arrived. I don't wish to be negative but make the most of that moment. Sadly, nothing lasts so enjoy it while it lasts. Don't take anything for granted and don't expect that your first job will lead on to one thing after another. Much as we would all like it to be the case, the business doesn't work like that.

What are the three golden tips you can give to someone going up for their first West End show?

I don't know what the golden tips are because, even after all this time, I'm still searching for them myself.

Looking back I suppose my success, such as it is, was based on always being really clear about the decisions I made before I went into any audition.

A clear choice of song is essential. Have a list of about five or six songs that show your voice off to its best and that are very different in feel and style from one another. Often you will be asked to bring a couple of contrasting songs to show off your vocal and playing range. The great thing about having a few songs that you know really well is that you will be intimate with the material but you can perform it in any number of different ways. It's very easy to change the intention of a song, not so easy to learn a new song for each audition you go up for.

Whatever it is that you are going up for think really carefully about the suitability of the song you are going to sing and make sure it is a good fit. Many people will say, 'try and sing something that they haven't heard time and time again'. It's a good point but if the song you choose is an old favourite try and do something different with that song.

Make a bold decision and stick with it!

I'll give you an example of what I mean: When I went for

my audition for 'Joseph And His Amazing Technicolored Dreamcoat' the show was more than 20 years old and the audition panel had heard the songs many, many times. I had to make a choice that would ensure that I stood out from all the others auditioning and make the song fresh and exciting.

Now, I was up for the part of the Narrator. It was all about the words and really colouring what I was singing about with clarity and energy. And then I had a bit of a brainwave. This is just storytelling to kids and when you're telling a story to children you really want to be on a level with them. So when I went into the audition I asked if I could have a chair because I really felt that I should be sitting down when I sang to them.

I sat down and started by picturing the children around me. I sang a bit of the prologue imagining their smiles. Doing that really helped me to bring the right amount of warmth and intimacy to the song at the same time capturing the imagination of the people auditioning me. It sounds simple but I was the only one to do it. And it must have worked because I got the job! I think in this particular instance I gave them something so clear that it worked in my favour.

Avoid the danger of being just like everyone else.

When I first started out there was a real sense of individuality. In my day, I feel the people who were most taken notice of and secured the work were always true to themselves but also bringing something new to the piece they were singing. When you heard me or Frances Ruffelle or Sally

Anne Triplett we all sounded different from one another, we had an honest organic sound and carried our own unique qualities with us whenever we sang. Now, you might not have liked what people were doing but there was no doubt about who was who and the style in which they sang.

I think nowadays, there is a tendency to listen to Idina Menzel and think that's how it got to be. I disagree. Yes listen to your musical theatre heroes but don't be tempted to just give a straight copy. Learn from them, of course, but make any song you sing your own. It is crucial that the people auditioning you get a sense of who you are and not just your ability to recreate a sound you've heard. Believe me there will be plenty of people doing that. If you want to stand out from the crowd, have the courage to be you.

When you are going up for a big role in a musical how should the performer prepare?

You must learn any material they send you inside out and back to front. Then, having learnt it you will know if the song is a comfortable sing or whether the range is too high for you, or indeed too low. If that is the case, take my advice; you will not be able to perform it eight times a week every week for a year.

If, in your heart of hearts you know a song is too difficult for you, pull out of the audition. Tough as it might seem, you won't be doing yourself any favours by going in and being seen to struggle with the technicalities of a song. Far better to come to terms with that fact with your singing coach than to audition badly and have the people auditioning you thinking poorly of you...because they will remember!

When you go into your audition they are likely to ask you to try the song in a number of different ways so it is essential that you are freed from any musical uncertainties that may have arisen when you were learning the piece. Also if you don't know the song absolutely 100% when you are given new direction, you are likely to forget it halfway through.

You started off your career playing leading roles. Can others expect this to happen to them?

For most people you can expect to work your apprenticeship. You will do your ensemble work, work your way up by doing cover work and then, if you're lucky you'll get the opportunity to audition for bigger and bigger parts. And to be honest, that is the best way.

There is so much more pressure that comes to bear when you are a principle player that to get acclimatised by working your way through the ranks will give you the requisite experience you need to cope. If I'm honest, I think there is a lot to be said for being an ensemble player and a brilliant cover without ever being cast in a principle role. It makes for an envied career in many ways. The pressures are far fewer but also you are practically guaranteed greater professional longevity.

If you only play leading roles and there is no leading role that is right for you what do you do then? Much as you might want to take small parts or ensemble work you can't because you would risk undermining your status within the business. If you are a jobbing musical performer there will be more work out there for you to enjoy and partake in. It is worth remembering, if you are lucky enough to be cast in a musical, however big or small you have done something amazing. You will be part of a tiny group of people ever to have done this and your achievement should never be diminished.

But what if you want to be a star?

When I started out all I wanted was to be in a musical. I didn't want to be a star I just wanted to be out there. In many ways I was very, very lucky to be in the right place at the right time, the right age, the right sex and the right height to be considered for the lead in Carrie and I was blessed to be cast.

For most performers a leading role will not happen and most leading players do not become stars in their own right. Being a performer should never be about wanting stardom. Those who come into this industry with that as their goal will almost certainly meet with heartache and disappointment. If you want to go into theatre do it because you love it and have to do it. If you want to earn lots of money or want to be recognised in the street go on Big Brother.

The bigger point to make here is that there are no musical theatre stars in this country. If you want personal notoriety you should go over to the States. Over there they love and nurture their musical performers. The Americans seem to have a higher regard for the art form and will cherish those individuals who have shone within the genre. Over here we love the spectacle, the music and the singing but the production will always outshine the individual.

This is a note for any actor/singers out there: Do not, under any circumstances, learn your songs from listening to a record and expect it to be the same as when you are singing with a piano accompaniment. You will be thrown and just end up looking like an amateur because, make no mistake about it something will go wrong. It might not be in the key you were expecting as what a performer chooses to sing on a cast recording might not be the notes a musical director will expect to hear. You will not have an intimate enough relationship to the song and the story you are trying to relate because you will not have rehearsed it properly.

Always take your songs to a good pianist and practice not the just the notes but where to breath, when to strengthen the sound, when to go softer, how long you want to sustain a note...The list goes on. There is no substitute for practicing your song with a proper musician and no excuse either.

You joined the business more than 25 years ago. What changes have you noticed in that time?

I think the main changes are just the sheer number of people who want to be in showbiz and (for those who avoid the trap of TV talent shows) just how well trained most people are.

In my day, you relied on your own uniqueness to shine through. I still think that is the most important element you can bring in to an audition but nowadays you've got to be able to read music, sing brilliantly, dance and act. You need grounding in all the elements that will make you a good prospect for employment. Given all that, the best piece of advice I can give is find something that you are really exceptional at and focus on it.

If you work to your strengths there will always be one area in which you shine. If you are more of an actor than a singer, concentrate on the acting element in a song. Of course we all love to hear a beautifully sung number but if a song is sung well but performed brilliantly you will be memorable.

You only have to think of Judi Dench's performance of Send in the Clowns in Sondheim's 'A Little Night Music' to know that it is one of the most powerfully performed songs you will ever see. Yet, it's not about the notes or the clarity of voice it's all about the words and the story she is telling with them.

My last question is, has it all been worth it?

Without a doubt. I know I have a tendency to harp on about the difficulties that the business throws at you- any experienced performer will always point out the hardships of being in the profession – but overall I have had the most incredible time.

Yes, it's a crazy game, but it has been good to me and I hope it is good to all the people who read this book. I have met some of the most incredible people who taught me so much about both life in the theatre and life in general. Those people have made me a much more open and rounded person while making the pleasure of working alongside them a quite simply amazing experience.

Yes, the business is full of injustices and hardships but, if you love it and you are committed to it 100%, there really is no business like show business.

Chapter 15

Auditioning for TV and film

In this chapter I have contributions from two fantastic and very successful screen actors. Karen Henthorn and Joseph Millson.

Karen has been on our screens since 1986 and for her 'second string' she works as a screen acting coach giving private one-to-one tuition and public workshops. She offers some highly effective techniques as well as highly informed opinion on how to audition for screen. But first, let me hand over to screen actor, Joseph Millson.

Joseph is one of our most enduring TV actors of the last 20 years. On screen he is well known for his leading roles in dozens of television series including Banished, 24: Live Another Day, Holby City, The Sarah Jane Adventures, Ashes to Ashes,

Eastenders and Peak Practice He has appeared in 14 feature films including Casino Royale, The Dead 2, Telstar, and the lead role in the soon to be released thriller, The Chameleon.

Get ready for some great advice, some hard truths and some truly valuable insights...

Auditioning for screen has become much tougher than it used to be when I started out 20 years ago. It strikes me that the time you are given for preparation is becoming so much less and, perversely what you are expected to bring to the room is so much more.

For a start, you will be expected to have thoroughly learnt it. There is just an innate frown in the room whenever you need to work from the page. One time in America during pilot season I totalled 12 meetings in one week. My learning responsibility was huge and I wracked up about 45 pages learnt in the space of one week.

The bottom line is you will not be taken anywhere near as credibly if you are not confidently off book.

The other difficulty from a technical point of view is that they won't send you the whole script so it is very difficult to know if you are taking the right approach to a character. If you were auditioning for Silence of the Lambs and you get one side with the lines, 'Hello Clarice, it's lovely to see you', you might well think, this bloke seems really nice. I play him with openness and warmth.

My big tip regarding this type of dilemma is that it is easier to jump from one solid rock to another with clarity and bravery instead of trying to jump out of the sea with your feet half in the sand. By that I simply mean, make solid decisions. Don't be wishy-washy. Make a choice and then play it 100%.

Directors tend to like those who come in with an idea even if it's wrong. Also if you have made one clear and strong character decision and go all out to play Hannibal Lector like he's a nice guy but the director then tells you that he is in fact a murdering psychopath, your mistake is easily remedied. In this situation the brain somehow finds it much easier to move from one solid place to another albeit very different than if you had gone in hedging your bets or not being sure what you were playing in the first place.

So even though playing Hannibal Lector as a nice guy was wrong at least you were committed and the director can see you were bold enough to make a choice. When he offers you some direction you will be able to respond to how he wishes you to approach it next time through. It all works in your favour.

Some brilliant advice from YouTube.

I saw a Youtube video featuring Bryan Cranston from 'Breaking Bad'. In it, he makes the point that you shouldn't go into an audition to 'get the job'. In his view getting the job is so far out of our hands that we shouldn't even bother considering it. Cranston maintains the best way to approach an audition is to go in and treat it as a performance. Not in a way that you are trying to please the audition panel by giving them what you think they want but more as an opportunity to do what we as actors love doing namely, acting.

If you view your audition as perhaps the only time you will get to play this part, enjoy playing it. Make strong decisions and have fun with it. In this way you will bring a terrific amount of detail to what you are doing, enjoy the acting of it while at the same time you will be empowering yourself. Serving the script is always better than simply looking for approval.

Clock up your mileage

I can't tell you how to get into an audition for TV or film except to say – work. And if that is taking a job in one pub theatre after another after another then do it. Be on your feet. Give people the chance to see you do what you love doing. Soon you will build up a body of work and, at some point somebody of influence will see you. Be that an agent, a casting director or a producer, it will eventually happen. There is a great phrase which holds true more in acting than any other field; 'The harder I work, the luckier I get'. Also, if you have experience in working in studio theatres the intimacy is very like what you will have with a camera when you are filming so it's beneficial in more than one way.

Also you should be 'clocking up your mileage' in any way possible. Nowadays, there is so much film and TV being made, *yes, a lot of it is low budget; some of it you will have to do for free (as in student films). My advice? No matter what the project or the fee get yourself in front of a camera and earn your spurs. Don't be snobbish about the script or the concept, get working. If the film turns out to be rubbish no one will ever see it and if it's good- Bingo!*

Look at the people in Star Wars. Most of the cast and crew had no idea of what the film would be like and few of them had much confidence that it would be any good. What could have been just another crappy sci-fi adventure makes history and all involved are garnered with laurels.

Student films are a brilliant way of getting yourself on a set. Clock up your miles. If nothing else, make your own mini movie. We all have the technology now to shoot with our smart phones and edit together our own film on our laptop.

If there are no opportunities coming your way make your own opportunities. Write something and film it. You never know where the experience and the end product may take you. Ben Affleck and Matt Damon won an Oscar for the screenplay of 'Good Will Hunting' (in which they also starred). Experience is vital and the more experience you have the more employable you become. Also solid experience will give you a confidence that you cannot fake.

Always serve your higher purpose

Keep your spirits up as best you can by falling in love with the life of a struggling actor. If you view everything you do through this prism then everything you do has a reason and the reason is your career.

Yes, you might have come away from a two-month job at a rep and end up serving coffee in a Starbucks - again! But if you know being a waiter in Starbucks is serving your higher purpose, then it's kind of cool and it will continue to feed the fire of your ambition.

The creative stuff is your responsibility

For the most part a first audition will be you, a casting director or one of their assistance and a camera. Now casting directors fulfil a hugely important role in the whole process of taking a film script and turning it into a reality. However, a lot of them won't necessarily be good readers. In fact it would be fair to say that some of them, by their own admission will be terrible readers. This is why you have to do all the creative work before you go into the room.

One thing to be aware of when you audition for screen, and this applies to both reading with casting directors and self tapes, is that in an effort to look suitably intense and impressive actors can often look as though they do not like the person they are reading opposite. And when producers and directors watch those tapes back it is very hard for them to see any of the actor's warmth or charm coming through.

Look for the window

Don't get me wrong, you might well be playing a character that lacks warmth or is in an argument but in those situations you must always find a point in the script where you can open up to the reader. Look for the little windows where you can find what they are saying genuinely funny and then return to being horrible.

When you are playing a scene with a character with whom you are supposed to be in love, be careful not to just play the intensity of the moment. When people look back at the tapes you will only be showing them one flavour of your personality. Again, look for the window where you can show a flash of warmth or affection.

I have helped cast a number of films and you wouldn't believe the number of people who play a love scene with a frown and they don't know they are doing it.

So... always look for the windows.

Watch your own work

Get your smartphone, stick it against the wall and tape yourself. Nowadays, we all have the technology to do this at no expense. Even if it is not a self-tape, film it yourself and watch it back. Look at what you think is good and keep it, check what you think doesn't work and make different choices.

Have a really simple objective

Once you strip away all the technical stuff about acting it all boils down to the fact that you can't play two things at once. Transitive verbs are a great way of mapping out a series of simple choices through a piece of script.

A transitive verb is one that comes inbetween the words 'I' and 'you'. Some simple examples might be;

I loath *you. I* suspect *you. I* mock *you. I* doubt *you. I* punish *you. I* seduce *you.*

It is very tempting to try and play the abstract past of a characters journey, his hatred of his mother, her life long suspicion of tall men. The truth is none of that can be seen by the camera, but a series of simple transitive verbs will help you give colourful and interesting choices that immediately inform the way you will say a line.

Don't try to improve poor writing

Here is a lovely tip that will take any sense of misplaced responsibility off the shoulders of an actor. If a script is rubbish, there is nothing you can do about it. Don't try to improve poor writing. You can't!

I had an audition for an American TV show coming up. I had the script sent over to me and after five minutes I found myself crossing things out and trying to change the odd line to suit my preference but I quickly had to remind myself that giving a script a rewrite is not my job.

It is my job to make a poor script as good as it can be by serving the writing no matter how bad it might be. Never make stuff up that isn't there, despite your best intentions, it just doesn't help!

Chose the money moment in a scene

Try and identify a moment in the scene where you are the next person to speak and take your time coming in with the line. Make it your moment. I promise you it will really stand out when the creatives revue the tapes. It is something that I do when I'm actually filming on a job too. We all know an editor can shorten a moment but they can't extend a look!

Casting directors hate this, so don't do it:

Needless to say this is not industry standard but in my experience things to avoid include sighing and putting 'look', 'You know' and 'I mean' before very line. Actors think they are making it more natural by putting these things in but it just tends to irritate.

The X Factor Psychology

One element that I think doesn't help young actors coming in to the business these days is what I call the X Factor psychology. By this I mean the expectation of fast and high achieving results.

It strikes me that people are more and more reluctant to

work their apprenticeship or indeed to see that as a worthwhile goal in itself. When I give lectures at various drama schools these days I will talk about my notion of 'clocking up your mileage' and before me I have a sea of faces and they're all thinking, 'f#ck that for a game of soldiers'.

One student piped up with the fact that a bloke he knew came out of drama school and his first job was on 'The Hunger Games'. My response was 'Well, bully for him. He will probably be less happy than someone who has built up their craft through years of working in the industry'. I often thank God that I didn't begin my career with a high profile movie job. Let's face it; unless you are supremely lucky that first job will probably mark the high point of your career. So it's over almost before it's started. I was 27 when I got my first big telly job but by that time I had clocked up 200 stage performances, about seven student films – I'd been shit in all of them but I was able to fail on a small stage not the world stage. By the time I was on the box I had gained sufficient experience and confidence to cope with, handle and thrive in the medium of television. Without that invaluable time on the road I would have made a fool of myself, I'm sure of it.

The X Factor mentality doesn't just affect young actors exclusively, I think it is an influence that we all have to beware of and actively choose to opt out of, for sake of our sanity as much as anything else.

Take whatever is going, learn from it and, over the years, grow into an actor of strength, self-assurance and experience.

Karen Henthorn has been working as a screen actress in both film and TV since 1986. Her credits include 'The Booze Cruise', 'EastEnders', 'The Street' by Jimmy Mc Govern as well as playing Tessa Bryant in 'Coronation Street' for two years. She recently played Janet Macy in 'In The Flesh' and Eileen in 'Pulling' for BBC3.

I have known Karen for many years and finally took the plunge and went for some screen acting classes with her. While I was with her I took the opportunity to ask a few questions on her approach to auditioning for the screen. Here she shares her views and experiences...

The greatest likelihood is that you will be rejected more often than you will be accepted for a job. Dealing with one or two things that don't go your way is a synch. After a year or two, not so easy! So how do we prepare for rejection? By knowing that you did your absolute best when you were in the room.

I know that it is a theme that is repeated often in this book but let me add my voice to the simple notion of learning your lines. Get that out of the way as soon as you can. And when you go into the audition take the script with you. For me, even though I know I've learnt my lines if I don't have my script with me I just know I'm going to forget it because nerves kick in! So I always take my script in with me and I always end up referring to it. If you need to refresh your memory between takes no one is going to mind. If however, you go in without your script and you forget something, it changes from being an audition into an exercise in remembering your lines.

If you are just trying to remember your lines in front of the director, the casting director maybe the producer as well, you will fail to listen, react, connect and be 'within the moment'. You will be viewed, quite rightly as someone working in a vacuum, like a rabbit in the headlights, just hoping to get through it without mucking it up. Ten out of ten for remembering it – a big fat zero for interpretation, character decisions, moments of truth and nuance.

Know that you truly know your lines, trust that your lines will be there for you and then you will enable yourself to start listening. If you think that you know your lines go through them while you are threading a needle or making the bed. If you forget them while doing something unrelated you need to go back and learn them more thoroughly.

I go through a number of stages when learning my lines. I learn them from the page, then I'll say them out loud, then I'll get someone to read with me and then I'll go for a walk while saying them out loud. People think I'm mad but what the hell!

An audition for screen is all about listening, it's about reacting, it's about being there, working off and working with your casting director or whoever it might be reading with you. So please, be as familiar as you possibly can be with your words.

Know about your relationship with the person you are

talking to in the scene. Go in with some choices and commit to them. They may not be the right ones but it shows the director that you have given it some thought. It might be that you have come up with an angle on the scene or character that the director hasn't thought about. If that is the case you will be bringing in so much to the room that it is hard for the director not to want to go further into the process with you by giving you some direction.

So, having said take decisions and commit to them you also have to be flexible enough to take what direction you are given and change what you are doing with no time to prepare what so ever. A way to help this flexibility is to learn your lines thoroughly but not rigidly. Don't learn your lines in a set pattern. If you only say your lines in one way, you will not be responding to the reader in the audition and that is really key. It's not acting it's reacting! Ideally you want an unbroken circle of energy between the two of you.

By not learning your lines in a set way you are more likely to be moved by your partner in the way they deliver their lines and the communication will flow between you.

During a one to one coaching session I will see my clients/students come in and start demonstrating their emotions instead of feeling them. A camera can spot someone 'acting' which is why your emotional decisions are so important when you do you preparatory work. Be careful of your vocal levels, people are always too loud in the first instance and often the piece I've asked them to prepare is rather flat and lacking in detail. So what I try to lead my student towards is personalising the material so that it means something to them, something that means something to them as an individual. You need to connect with that, trust that, talk about it (even if it's to yourself) in doing this you will bring depth to the line and the work transforms. They have now made an internal connection to the meaning, the feeling and the thought for that line.

One of the difficulties I and most actors face is that they don't get a great deal of time in front of the camera to grow in confidence and hone their screen acting skills. That's why I loved my time on Coronation Street so much. Not only because my character was so vile and fun to play, but because, above everything else, I was working in my chosen profession every day for eighteen months solid. It was a wonderful environment. Yes, you're being stretched by the day to day rigours of the shooting schedule but it was a great place to take risks and try ideas out. Katherine Kelly, (a fantastic actress who uses her space so beautifully) who played Becky, gave me a wonderful piece of advice.

Before I actually started the job she took me to one side and said, 'if you want to try something out in a scene and it doesn't work – don't worry about it. You've got another scene and another and another. You've got another 18 months worth of scenes so enjoy yourself, take risks and go for it'. I couldn't get my head around it at first. I thought, 'oh my God, it's got to be *spot on every time 'cos it's television and so many people see it'. But doing something like a soap does give you the opportunity to explore and experiment.*

Katherine made the point that the general public tend not to latch onto the things actors will find frustrating in their own performance. It was great to have the freedom that time gave on a long contract to try new things out.

The other lovely thing about being so long on one job was that I had no financial worries for some considerable time. I skipped to work every day, I knew I was earning a living and those two things hand in hand lifted the weight of every day woes off of my shoulders within an instant. The constant worries of 'when's the next audition' or 'where's the rent coming from for next month' vanished. All I had to do was show up on time having learnt my lines. And learning lines ain't no worry!

If you live in the Manchester area or are prepared to make the journey please go and see Karen for your screen acting classes. She is a total expert, a force of nature and a first class tutor; compassionate, challenging, honest and supportive. Look her up online – www.karenhenthornscreenacting.com

Actor Alan Turkington has put together a highly instructive piece on the best way to make a 'Self Tape' audition. Bearing in mind just how prevalent this type of screen audition is becoming, scour the next few pages and act on the information within them.

How To Compose a 'Self Tape' audition

Self-taping is now becoming more and more common as the first step in preliminary auditions for both TV and film. Legendary casting director Roz Hubbard was recently talking about this on Radio 4 and said it was all to do with budgets being cut from the casting process but, in fairness, with modern filming technology becoming so very good and with quite literally everybody having that technology at their disposal to self tape to an industry acceptable standard why not?!

On the down side it could be argued that we have been given a responsibility that the production company should provide but more positively, no matter how badly you may do on the first take you can chose to reshoot as many times as you like and only submit once you are really happy with your take. Also, it means that you are always available for that first round audition no matter where you are in the country or, indeed, the world. You can, of course, use the service offered by Spotlight or Take 5 Casting where you pay in the region of £30-50 for half an hour with a room and a reader if you're really stuck.

In light of these changes, I have compiled a list of taping recommendations suggested to me by actors who have really got into the groove of the self-tape phenomenon to assist you in achieving the highest level of quality in your auditions. When these things were first being produced by actors nobody had a clear idea of what the standard of 'production values' should be and how to best package and share the end clip. I hope to give you a few really helpful pointers to get you started.

The idea of this list of suggestions is not to overload you with technical requirements but more to simplify the process down to what is both acceptable and strictly necessary. I know that when I first self taped I got carried away and made the whole thing into a short film worthy of being shown in art house cinemas across the land with what I thought were appropriate locations, a few ambient sound effects and even a rolling credit at the end. I sent it off thinking how clever I was and how it was bound to catch the eye of the casting director. How wrong I was. I was later told that all the whistles and bells just acted as an irritating distraction.

If, like me, you are a bit of a whizz on an iMovie editing suit please take this first suggestion to heart.

1: You are doing a simple self-tape. You are not making a movie. Keep it as simple as possible and let your performance be the thing that gets you through to the next round. Many actors choose to invest in a small digital camera, but the camera on your smartphone will more than suffice. As well as this the next 'must' is a small tripod with a grip that will clamp around your phone. This shouldn't cost more than about £10-20 and Joby's Gorillapod is as good an idea as any as you can attach its trademark bendy legs to something at eye level.

2: With regard to lighting I was once given the instruction from a casting director that it "should be good enough so we can see the colour of the actor's eyes", though I have found this a pretty impossible task. As a rule of thumb, use soft lighting if possible – avoid stark white light.

3: At the beginning of your tape please do not use the black fade in and out feature on your camera. According to a casting director friend of mine this makes cutting together a collection of people's self tapes difficult to edit when it comes to compiling a short list to pass onto the producers. As a general rule you should never see black on your tapes at the beginning or end of your auditions.

4: Start each audition with framing that shows the actor's head and shoulders only. Tape should lead with audition first and then a slate at the end.

5: The sound must be clear. Interestingly if your video is not of the best quality from a visual point of view people will still be happy to watch it – as long as they can hear it. If it's the other way round, perfect visual image but poor sound they will switch you off almost immediately so we must make sure the sound on our tape is clear and of good quality. If you want to spend a few quid and really up the spec on this you can buy a microphone for your smartphone. The enhancement will be quite noticeable but in all fairness the condenser mic on your phone will easily be good enough as long as there are no loud or irritating background noises going on.

6: If you are reading a two handed scene (you will be) it is imperative that the person reading the other part STANDS BACK from the microphone so as not to overpower the actor's voice. The actor's voice should be clearly heard and the reader's should be quieter.

7: Please tape auditions in front of a light-coloured, solid wall or backdrop. Try not to have anything behind the actor that will distract the viewer's eye, like furniture, pictures, windows, etc. Again, a clean, solid wall or backdrop is best. This is one of the mistakes I made. I chose a location with a beautiful view out to beautifully manicured gardens, which I thought would help set the scene. In the first instance it confused the iris on my camera by giving it two light sources to chose between so I came out a bit orange and in the second, it only served to crowd the shot.

8: Only submit one good take. I would suggest only putting forward a second if you feel really strongly about showing a different creative choice and it is a good read. But be warned you could be in danger of undermining yourself. A second take might suggest that you don't quite have enough faith in your original submission.

9: At the end of your take, each actor should slate his/her name and the role they are reading for with head and shoulders framing. 'Slating' a shot is one of those lovely US terms (!) but just means 'name and agent to camera'. For some roles (particularly US roles) they will want to know your height at this point too, but this will usually be specifically asked for.

10: At the end of your self tape you should pull back for one, quick, full body shot.

11: It is acceptable to use a simple title block that shows actor name, role and agency at the very beginning of the tape. I quite like this option. While I don't want you to fall into the trap of thinking you are Fellini – a little polish can go a long way. There are some great simple 'titles' in iMovie, but again, stay away from the fancy ones and make sure there's not a fade-in to your audition piece (ie. in iMovie, don't use a 'Transition').

12. With regard to uploading it to the casting director, there are two main ways and the casting director will specify which they prefer. Either upload the file to wetransfer.com and file share it with the casting director, or register with vimeo.com (posh Youtube) and upload it to 'your videos' there, but MAKE SURE you password protect it. Once this is uploaded to vimeo, vimeo sends you the link to it and you can email the casting director with this (and the password). I prefer to use Vimeo as you can keep all your self-tapes together (wetransfer only keeps them for a week) and recently I was unable to attend an on-the-day audition, but was able to point the director towards a couple of previous self-tapes on

my Vimeo page.

As self-taping is becoming so mainstream you can book yourself on self tape courses, though these are rather ad hoc at the moment and it is a matter of keeping abreast of courses at The Actors Centre. The Irish casting director Maureen Hughes has rather taken a lead on this with a module at her Bow Street Theatre school in Dublin.

Chapter 16

Auditioning for theatre

Our chosen expert contributor for this chapter is my co- author Richard Williams.

As well as running a course at The Drama Centre London I am a theatre director of some 35 years' experience. Auditioning professional actors has given me the chance to meet all sorts of performers at all sorts of different stages of their careers. While most auditions have run in a pretty predictable way there have been a few which have stuck in my mind, not necessarily for the best reasons.

We have spoken at great length about what you can do to give a great audition, but it is worth saying that in the mad artificiality of the audition room actors who have tried to do their best have often gone completely off the rails. I want to give you a few examples from auditions I have held in the past of what not to do.

Directors very often talk about wanting to work with actors who bring a sense of danger with them to the stage, however there is a big difference between bringing a sense of excitement to the performance and coming over as a lunatic in the auditions.

Occasionally actors go crazy in auditions – so be warned, and if you find yourself doing these sorts of things it's probably better to take a rest!

Waiting for Vittoria

A very long time ago I was auditioning in one of the cheapest audition venues in London – The Abbey Community Centre (which was demolished years ago). The room was L shaped with the door in the short bit of the L. I was seated at the end of the long bit of the L furthest away from the door. There was a window at either end of the long bit of the L.

A middle aged actor came in and as we talked he revealed he had been an architect until he was 40 and had recently turned to acting. I asked what his most recent job had been and he said he had been at the Northcott Theatre, Exeter in an adaptation of a Sherlock Holmes story. I asked what he'd played and he said it was some lord or other. As I didn't know the story I asked if it was a good part. He said it was and, in the spirit of encouraging him, I asked what was it that made it good. He replied it was because the character didn't appear until the final five minutes of the play. I was confused and asked why that made it a good part. He looked at me clearly astonished. Then he said rather testily, 'It was good because I was already down on stage for the curtain call'. So I knew I was now alone in a room in central London with at the very least, an eccentric.

I cut through the rest of the usual chat and asked him what his audition speech was. 'I'll do Montecelso's arraignment of Vittoria from The White Devil, by Webster', he said. I felt reassured. A great speech from the court scene when The Cardinal accuses Vittoria of being a whore. Strong meaty stuff. I felt we were back on track. The actor went down the room and instead of turning to face me, as I expected, he disappeared round the corner of the L shape. There was then a series of crashing noises as chairs fell over and other miscellaneous stuff fell to the floor. A moment or two later he reappeared with a hat stand which he placed in the middle of the room. 'This is Vittoria', he explained. OK so far. He then disappeared from my sight by going round the turn of the room off stage were he started the speech. I thought. 'He'll enter in a moment.' But he didn't – the speech went on at some length as the Cardinal 'expounded whore' and I sat looking at the hat stand. I was hearing a radio version of the play and was auditioning a hat stand!

It was worrying. I was alone and it could be hours before my bleeding body would be discovered. I needed to get him out. The speech ended and he came round the corner anxiously asking, 'How was I?' 'Very good and many thanks,' I said, *ushering him towards the door. 'What about my contemporary speech?' He said this in a rather malicious tone so as much for my own safety as anything else I said, 'Yes well if it isn't too long...'*

'It's from Waiting for Godot,' he said. 'Godot?' I thought. The lines are only a few words long, it's all that quick fire repartee? What does he mean?

'It's Lucky's speech.' My God. Lucky's speech! It's pages long and is utterly incomprehensible philosophical raving! But he'd started. There he was raving around, frothing at the mouth three feet away! A simple move and he could have strangled me!

I now felt something I had never felt before or since in an audition. I felt I was going to laugh out loud. The madness of the situation had got to me. First the hat stand and now the spitting and slobbering, and the growing fear that I was going to be found dead or at least badly wounded several hours later. The laughter was mounting inside. The moment when I would laugh and he would become a homicidal lunatic was fast approaching. Just as the two were about to collide inspiration came, a gestalt moment. I would laugh, he would stop and in outrage move towards me and I would say, and this was genius, 'I'm so sorry. It wasn't you or your speech. I glanced through the window behind you and saw a person mooning from a nearby building, but they've gone now!' It might buy me enough time to get out.

I never needed to use it because just as I was about to break down in laughter he leered at me in the most alarming way and ran out of the room, cursing and swearing at me, and all directors.

Skiing

On another occasion I had a very good chat to a young female actor who was entirely normal and charming. I was sitting behind a desk and when I asked her to do her speech she explained it was about skiing and the character was skiing downhill. At this point she got up, stood on her chair and then stepped onto the table I was sitting at. She launched into her speech doing appropriate skiing actions. Her knees were about four inches from my face. She was wearing jeans so it wasn't embarrassing, but it was pretty odd to be auditioning a pair of knees!

Twelfth Night or Why Would You Do that?

A very serious, young actor came in and we had the normal sort of chat. He was pleasant enough but very serious. He told me he would be doing a speech from Twelfth Night and had decided to do Viola's Ring Speech. OK so cross gender speech, why not? Then he started. He spoke incredibly, incredibly slowly and as he spoke incredibly slowly he walked to the wall and then turned to face the wall, and addressed the wall as he slowly sidestepped round the room, facing the wall throughout.

I'm sure every director has dozens of stories about the madness that overcomes actors in the craziness of the audition and the horrible feeling the actor has of wanting to leave a mark, to be memorable. Sadly the mad and memorable don't get the work. Reliable, intelligent, hardworking and well prepared are some of the qualities which might get you through the audition process, but nothing is certain except uncertainty. For this reason I can't help thinking that a good phrase for an actor to keep in mind is 'Tolerate Uncertainty!'

Going from negative audition experiences to the most impressive audition I have ever seen...

I was holding interviews for a new musical called 'Sadly Solo Joe' which, coincidently, co-author Paul wrote (he is multi talented as you have no doubt discovered). We had a day of auditions scheduled and as is the custom the casting director sent out a few pages of the script for people to take a look at and read when they came in. The pages had been sent out during the previous afternoon. We saw a lot of good people, mostly from successful West End musicals, who sang and read brilliantly. Then at midday an actress called Hanna Waddingham came in.

We chatted, she sang and then I asked her to read. She stood up and without reference to the printed script acted the scene effortlessly. She had received the script during a matinee of the show she was appearing in the previous afternoon, and had learnt it perfectly between the matinee and the evening performance. She was bright, intelligent and showed her work *ethic by her actions. And, it goes without saying, she was terrific. Not surprisingly she was offered the part. Not surprisingly she had a stack of conflicting possibilities. How could anyone not be impressed by that level of commitment?*

Auditioning has changed over the years. In the 70s and 80s (and a bit into the 90s), in the golden age of the regional theatres in Britain, directors would personally do all the casting and the major responsibility was to engage a company of actors for a season, each of them playing a variety of roles over the period of about nine months. The company would probably be augmented now and then with guest actors, but the company was the backbone of the regional repertory theatre network. The job of the director at this time was to recruit a versatile bunch of actors who could take on a Shakespeare, an Ayckbourn, a Christmas show with songs, a new play, a West End style comedy and a modern classic like Shaw or even Brecht. It was the place where young actors got real experience, working with older actors and playing a wide spectrum of parts. The levels of pay made it possible for actors to have a mortgage, run a car and sometimes enjoy a drink!

What has changed? Well, practically everything is more expensive. The housing shortage, high rents and the basic expectations which are higher. Also there are so many more options in film, video, corporate work and so on. The relative levels of pay have fallen and so the majority of the regional theatres now operate as partly receiving houses, partly as members of groups of co-producers and then once in a while, as resources allow, staging their own productions.

In this circumstance the role of the artistic director has diminished and the administrator has morphed into a chief executive who is more and more the person who decides policy. The other big change is that casting directors are much more common, even with small companies. Artistic directors have always had a heavy workload, and perhaps didn't get out to see as many shows, with actors in action, as the casting director who is dedicated to seeing actors at work. On the other hand it's another hoop for actors to jump through, but perhaps a beneficial hoop.

In terms of auditioning, the search for the more versatile actor might appear to have become a thing of the past. However, counter intuitively, that isn't always the case. While the longer contract for a season is far less common, the nature of theatre has changed. The kind of plays I outlined above were all 'talking plays' or at least the style of production generally put emphasis on the delivery of the text.

The slogan was 'the primacy of the text'! Today there is a clear emphasis on the physical dimension of theatre even if not specifically 'physical', and this in turn often requires actors to produce music. So playing an instrument, having some idea of your own physical abilities, singing, and so on are all skills worth brushing up or even starting to learn. Actors need to have the agility to move with the times and the fashions in production. I remember the time when lots of actors were learning Welsh because it was clear that Channel 4 in Wales would be needing a good supply of Welsh speaking performers.

The opportunities that the regions offered in the past have been replaced by a huge growth in small companies based not just in London but throughout the country. Usually working on very tight budgets, there is terrific variety of presentation from companies like Theatre Delicatessen's site specific shows, Pants On Fire's physical and musical mini epics, through Filter's gloriously wild Shakespeare to the rediscoveries of older plays and championing of new work at The Finborough for example. So it would be wrong to be pessimistic. There is a lot of work going on, but it's in changed circumstances and it requires actors to be ever more flexible.

Conversely there is also a tendency to cast rather severely to type. Just be prepared for a director to tell you that the character is 32 so at 35 you're unsuitable. Just make sure you're there when that director is casting a 35 year old! How will you know? - by keeping a keen eye and ear and keeping in touch with your agent.

So what are the requirements for any actor, attending a professional audition? In terms of presenting skills it's vital that the actor stresses all and every talent. Acting, singing, dancing, physical skills – they're all requirements for the successful stage actor today. As always you shouldn't pretend you have skills you don't actually possess, but you can highlight any additional talents. My advice is to take singing lessons, revive those piano lessons and pull out the leotard and tights for some intensive dance classes.

On the question of not lying about your abilities, I remember an actor telling me, rather shamefacedly, that he had told a TV director he could drive a bus. He couldn't, so it wasn't a surprise to anyone, except the director, when he was later booked to play a coach driver on Coronation Street and, in ignorance, reversed the coach into the camera, completely destroying the camera, nearly killing the cameraman and thus ensuring he never worked for Granada TV again.

So here's a checklist for stage auditioning. You might be surprised at some of the comments, but these are the things I've noticed over decades of auditioning. You might think you don't commit any of these mistakes, but take time to check. Over a period of time you might have lost some of that enthusiasm which people warmed to a few years earlier.

1. Make sure you don't come across as a malcontent. Chose to talk about things in a positive way. No-one likes a moaner.

2. Make sure you don't come across as a nut case. There are plenty of those in the acting profession, so don't go along in a cowboy hat or a tutu.

3. Be on time at the right place. You can check addresses on the internet and agents can be vague about the details. Being ditzy doesn't cut it.

4. Agents are sometimes poor at getting details of the plays

or projects. Ask for as much detail as you can and use it to prepare. Directors and casting directors get tired of, 'My agent didn't really know what this is about.'

5. Do as much research as possible on the play, the writer and the people you're going to see. Not so much to work in a bit of flattery about them, as to avoid falling into an elephant trap, as you blather about hating 'In Your Face' drama only to discover later that the person you met has built a career on it.

6. Remind yourself of the last theatre you did, or the last play you saw and liked. Directors tend to be divided into stage and screen, and can sometimes guard their chosen territory jealously, so don't let them think you only occasionally go to the theatre or cinema.

7. Do a little vocal warm up before you go in. It's amazing how much croaking and spluttering goes on from people who are in the communication business!

8. What is a director looking for? Energy and enthusiasm, intelligence and individuality, good humour and good will.

9. Don't ask about the money! It's amazing how often this happens and most directors don't deal with the money, and if they do the audition isn't the right place to discuss it. Of course if the director brings it up then you will talk about it.

10. Don't apologise about not having worked for a time. Everyone knows that even the best people have spells out of work. Don't draw attention to it.

In chapter 3 Paul has spoke about the need for a robust second string but just to add my tuppence worth:

What every actor needs these days, when actors are many, jobs are few and money is scarce, is a secondary interest or job. You could follow Paul and become a top line personal coach in presentation skills, you could become a web designer, you could work for a charity which understands the special arrangements actors need for auditions and leave to go filming or be in a play, be a taxi driver or supply teacher, a decorator or carpenter or anything else which fits the bill. If you play a musical instrument you have a ready-made source of income.

There is a presentation guru on YouTube TED talks called Mark Bowden. He coaches international executives and United Nations' representatives, guess what? He started out as an actor with an interest in physical theatre and body language which eventually led him onto coaching. He is now one of the leaders in his field. You may not have even thought about this but there are other things in life as rewarding as acting!!

But the point is that every actor has periods out of work and you need some way of making money, which isn't boring or at worst humiliating. You want to find something which either pays amazing amounts of money or is creative in some way.

One thing that the majority of actors fail to realise let alone act on is the notion that as creative people everyone can reinvent themselves in a way that is impossible in most other careers. As an actor you can take the decision to write a play for yourself and your friends (The League of Gentlemen for example). Actor Simon McBurney when not appearing in films such as 'Mission Impossible' and 'Tinker Tailor Soldier Spy' runs the internationally renowned Theatre de Complicité which he formed back in the early 80s. A final example of this is an actress called Linda Marchall who during a down-time in her acting career started writing. In an effort to keep her acting and writing careers separate she changed her name to Linda La Plant – She went on to create one of the greatest detective series of the last 30 years – Prime Suspect. Once you notice it you can't help being struck by the number of actors who write and/or direct. If they can do this so can you.

On my course at The Drama Centre London I have a thread called Writing/Directing. The idea is to suggest to the students that they might have other talents which they could build on as a natural compliment to acting.

Shelagh was an actor who, 20 years ago, was bumping along with small acting jobs here and there. I hadn't seen her for years when I saw a poster for a feature film with her name as the screenwriter. By coincidence I met her at a party a few months later. 'How did you get to write a feature film?' I asked her. 'I had an idea for a radio play and wrote it. I wrote it. That was the secret. I didn't start it and give up. I wrote it. The rest just followed.'

Writing, directing, casting are all creative roles and you

might combine them with an acting career.

When it's good, acting is the most exciting and rewarding occupation. A nice group of creative people, social life provided, the possibility of the film winning an award or the play transferring. What could be better? Well nothing much – when you are actually acting. The gaps in between are killers and they often make your appearance at the next audition increasingly stressful. But you must remember as an actor you are never alone in this frustration. Your plight is a well-known part of a profession made up of wonderfully creative supportive and understanding people. Your job is to remain optimistic and fully prepared at all times to go in to your next audition and grab it by the scruff of the neck. It really is all up to you.

Chapter 17

Auditioning for commercials

I have auditioned for countless commercials over the last 38 years, at a guess maybe 400 or so. Out of those I got Eveready Batteries, Kentucky Fried Chicken, McDonald's (x2), Burger King, The Daily Mirror, Vauxhall, Renault, Ford, Nissan, DFS (x6) Central Massif, Spanish Rail, Heineken, Carte D'Or Ice Cream, Warburton's Bread a Spanish bank and about another 30 or so that I can't even remember!

All the above make me the expert contributor for this

chapter. Good to be back!

The first thing to say about commercial castings is that it is a numbers game. The more you are seen for the better chance you get of converting. Looking at the above list and only thinking about it for the first time as I write I suppose my strike rate has been pretty good over all. About one in ten. I would think that is a good average to aim for.

You might get lucky and get a big one straight away or you might go for loads and get nothing for years but it is worth remembering that this part of the business is more like the lottery than any other. You have to be in it to win it!

What are the rewards?

As I have already said, the money on commercials has been hit very hard by the market forces at play in the way adverts are screened and viewed, so the rewards are not as lip-smacking as once they were. Having said that, as Joseph Millson said, you can't buy audition experience you have to experience it and a commercial casting is a great way to allow yourself to be bold and brave in your decisions while auditioning. Also, while the money isn't what it was, commercials are a great way to travel for free! Yes, I have shot some in the wilds of West London and the docks of the East End but I have also seen America, Spain, The Virgin Islands, Greece, Italy, Norway, Denmark, Germany, Belgium and Paris all as a result of booking the right commercials!

What is required?

Oddly, commercial casting directors are very specific in the people they call in. This is largely due to the detail provided to them by the client. The good thing about this is that you know before you turn up that you are in with a shout. Don't be surprised though if you are a five foot two cheeky chappy being seen alongside a tall rather serious fellow and a tubby avuncular type. You will all be right for the role but the casting director needs to provide a wide range of options to the client. It is very easy to talk yourself out of getting an advert because you think you don't fit the type required. Don't second guess your casting director, trust them; they know what they are doing.

For this reason I always think that it is best to be as 'me' as I can when I go up for an ad. They are looking for individual types with an individual take on what is required in the casting so as there is nothing more unique than me I concentrate my efforts on allowing my personality to come through.

One of the refreshing elements to a commercial casting is that there is little or no preparation to be done. Even if you have to learn lines it will only ever be a few lines. And guess what I'm about to say now...when you are given your sides do your best to learn them as you wait to go in. It just helps to make you stand out not just to the director when he reviews the tapes but to your casting director.

If I was to put my success in commercial castings down to

one thing it would be that I proved myself to be a very dependable performer whenever I go for an advert.

I suggest that you be as good-humoured and artistically flexible as possible. Come up with ideas and sell them to the camera each time you do a take.

What casting directors want is someone who is going to provide something instantly and have the ability to take direction there and then without too many questions. 'What's my motivation?' is one you should avoid when auditioning for an advert.

When a casting director knows that you have the ability to think on your feet and create novel and appropriate ideas from the instructions they have given you they will bring you in again and again and THAT is when you have a chance of booking an advert. Like I said, it's all about the numbers in this particular sector of the business.

By making yourself dependable, flexible and surprising you will stay in the mind of your casting director and you will cultivate a working relationship that has the potential to last for years.

Thinking on your feet

Your improvisational skills are really going to come as an essential skill here. I once did a commercial where the camera was hoisted on a cherry picker from the outside of a building and peered in through the window to discover me picking my nose. We shot it more than 40 times and each time they wanted something different - a change in attitude, level of surprise, of embarrassment, indignation, mischievousness, whatever. When they go to the editing room they need as many alternatives as possible to choose from.

In your casting you can expect at least a couple of runs at it, often more, with a different direction each time. Go as wholeheartedly as you can with what they ask you to do.

There are a few industry acknowledged things that casting directors don't want from their actors and you would be well advised to check these out. If you notice this type of behaviour in yourself change it.

Being late!

Casting directors hate this for all the obvious reasons. It slows things down, puts them out and knocks on to every one else's time.

I always aim to arrive about 15 or 20 minutes before my slot. For commercials there can be anything up to three forms to fill in before you can go through to your casting. Yes, it's boring but it's a fact of life so get used to having to sit a GCSE every time. Also you must give yourself time to review whatever script there might be. Often it is just a storyboard with a few notes but you need to digest this and if you only have time to hurriedly fill in your forms you are spending your waiting time on the wrong thing.

Changing your time slot!

We spoke about this earlier with agent Bill Petrie but just to reiterate this point - if a casting director is seeing fifteen people for a casting in one afternoon and three of them ask to change their slot everything goes completely t#ts up! Best practice here is to go with what you're given. If you shift your slots too many times you will be annoying both your casting director and your agent.

Being grumpy!

For some reason, maybe it is the time keeping element (some commercial castings run horribly late) but actors are known to sit and huff and puff and be rather surly as they wait for a commercial auditions. There is no doubt about it, any arrangements you might make after your casting should be given plenty of room for flexibility. It is just the nature of the beast with commercial castings that they can start late and often run over. The worst I ever experienced was two and-a-half hours! That is a long time in anybody's book but if you can't wait with good grace then leave, or if you have a pressing engagement elsewhere tell the casting assistant, they will do what they can to help you out.

Being haughty!

Some actors feel the need to telegraph how above it all they are in their attitude to the casting assistant and all those who are sitting in the waiting room with them. It might be that certain actors think that commercials are beneath them. I don't know they might be, but if that is the case, tell your agent not to put you up for them. On the other hand take care. If you use Amanda Tabak at Candid Casting as an example she casts many adverts but also loads of TV and films too. Remember what Bill Petrie said about how many castings you are cutting yourself out of by not going through the door.

I was chatting with a commercial casting agent about this negative mindset that actors often come in with.

'If they don't want to be there fine, leave. By putting out this negative vibe they are affecting everyone else in the room. Commercial castings are two things at once; low stress and high pressure. I need my actors to be relaxed and positive but at the same time focused on giving of their best when they are in the room and any type of ego based negative behaviour can deflate others as they wait and more crucially play with their heads in a way that is not conducive to giving a good audition.'

In my view commercial castings are a serious business that actors shouldn't take too seriously. On the serious side, arrive on time, be friendly, do your best. On the not serious side, don't over think things and go on about the rest of your day happy knowing that it went as well as you could have hoped.

Again, more than in any other area of the business, the reasons why you get – or don't get a commercial range from between arcane and downright chaotic! The decision making process that the client goes through depends on so many variables, personal tastes and boardroom power playing that it is amazing a decision is ever actually reached or a commercial is actually shot and finally broadcast!

There's another reason not to take commercials too seriously. With a normal audition the final decision is out of your hands. In a casting for a commercial it is out of everybody's hands and seemingly rests in the lap of the Gods. Your ability as an actor, your talent as a performer and your warmth and value as an individual count for nothing when it comes to who is finally chosen, so it is very important that you don't sweat the result in any way.

If you get your ad fantastic! You might earn £1,600 or £8,000 or £12,000! You might be really lucky and get an old fashioned repeats fee deal and make a great deal of cash – they still exist but they are rare. You might be shooting in someone's house on the edge of Clapham Common but you might be whisked off for a few days to Venice or Johannesburg – you just never know.

If you don't get your ad? Chillax. If you have gone in with the right attitude you will be seen again and again and again...

Be Warned!

Getting an advert does not mean you will be shooting your advert. I got an advert for a German video product but they asked if I would be happy to fly out to Hamburg for a 'final audition' where I would be seen alongside another actor before the client would finally decide. I was happy to go along for the ride which is what it turned out to be in the end as they went with the other guy!

Another time, without being forewarned I turned up to film a British Gas advert only to find that myself and another actor would be filming it leaving the final decision to be taken when both actors could be compared in the finished article! That went well for both of us. He got Scotland and I got the United Kingdom but it still wasn't nice.

Be Warned – part two!

Shooting an advert does not mean you will ever see the advert- or ever earn the money!

This happened to me once and only once. I shot a high end, very glossy commercial that was to be part of a huge nationwide campaign. The shooting fee totalled about £700 - nice, but the real payday was to come when it went to air. Which didn't happen! Well over £10,000 that didn't come my way. Hard news to swallow particularly a week before Christmas but hey ho! I mention it not to brood (after I had cried my eyes out for a year or two I was surprisingly philosophical about it) but more as a salutary warning. I was spending the money long before it hit my account (only figuratively thank God!). I would hate anybody out there to run up debt on a credit card as they waited for money from a commercial to come in and end up in trouble. Only spend it when you've got it.

Adverts are great though

For most actors the getting of a commercial comes as a welcome shot in the financial arm with the bonus of a free holiday if you're really lucky. Of course no actor wants to just do ads but I would say they have their place, they have their worth, they can provide you with fantastic filming experience and they can lead to other things.

Epilogue

Both Richard and I hope we have given you some strong insights and practical advice that you can work with to improve your chances of being more regularly employed and enjoying a rich and varied long-lasting acting career.

We would like to leave you with one final thought:

One of the challenges for everyone who chooses acting as a career is that when you look out from your own situation you generally only see people in their successful moments. So you might think of Jeremy Irons living in a castle in Ireland starring in Hollywood blockbusters but forget that he started out as an ordinary jobbing actor (one of his first jobs was in a BBC children's TV show called Play Away). The challenge is to hold onto the promise of everything that an acting career offers without becoming cynical during those inevitable periods when things don't seem to be going your way.

We wish you the very best of luck in this nonsensical business of ours and sincerely hope that you do indeed audition your way to success.

Now go get 'em!

42066051R00133

Made in the USA
Middletown, DE
14 April 2019